Word 97 for Windows Workbook
Advanced

by Paul Summers

Software Training Workbooks
16 Nursery Road
Pinner
Middlesex
HA5 2AP

ACKNOWLEDGEMENTS

The author would like to thank Sally Walker for editing the exercises and suggestions for improving the book.

Cover art work by Paul Ostafiehyk @ St. Paul's Reprographics.

ISBN 1-90228-106-3

Published by:
Software Training Workbooks
16 Nursery Road
Pinner
Middlesex
HA5 2AP

Printed by St. Paul's Reprographics, 35 St. Paul's Close, Ealing Common, London, W5 3JQ.

CONTENTS

INTRODUCTION

EXERCISES

ADDITIONAL EXERCISES

APPENDIX

[THIS IS A BLANK PAGE]

INTRODUCTION

TO START WORD

If you have a menu on the screen follow the instructions to start Word 97.

 If you have Windows click on the **Start** button, point at the **Programs** option, then click on the **Microsoft Word** option in the programs group.

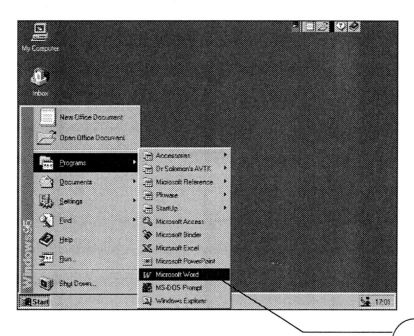

Only now should you place your disc in the floppy drive (A:).

Click the **Microsoft Word** option in the Programs group.

NEW, SAVE, PRINT AND CLEAR YOUR DOCUMENT

**PROPERTIES
WINDOW**

If the Properties
window appears
after you have
clicked to save
the file simply
click **OK** again.

TO OPEN A NEW DOCUMENT
Select **File**, **New**, highlight the **General** tab, highlight the **Blank
Document** template, select to Create New **Document**, and then
click **OK**
N.B. *Usually, selecting File, New and OK is all you will need
to do.*

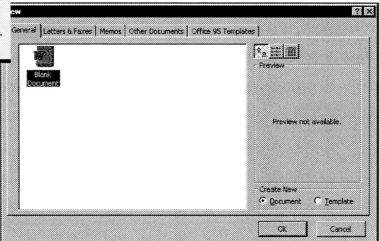

TO SAVE YOUR DOCUMENT
Select **File** and then **Save**
Click in the **File name** box and then enter the name of
your document as **TEST**
Select to Save in the **3 ½ Floppy (A:)** drive
Click the **Save** button

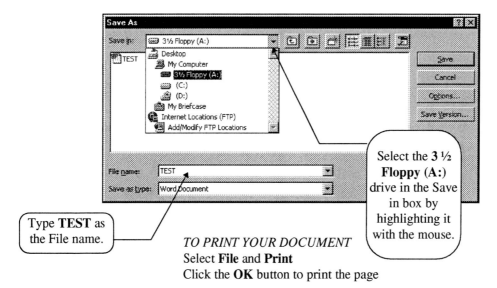

Type **TEST** as
the File name.

Select the **3 ½
Floppy (A:)**
drive in the Save
in box by
highlighting it
with the mouse.

TO PRINT YOUR DOCUMENT
Select **File** and **Print**
Click the **OK** button to print the page

TO CLEAR THE SCREEN
Select **File** and then **Close**

by Paul Summers

CURSOR MOVEMENT

PgDn	Down one screen
PgUp	Up one screen
Home	To the beginning of the current line
End	To the end of the current line

PRESS THESE KEY COMBINATIONS CONSECUTIVELY

PRESSING TWO KEYS AT ONCE

Always HOLD down the first key (*Ctrl*) and then PRESS the second key (*Home*) once.

Ctrl Home	Start of document
Ctrl End	End of document
Ctrl →	Word right
Ctrl ←	Word left

N.B. *The Ctrl key is sometimes labelled Control.*

DELETION

Delete	Deletes the character to the right of the cursor
Backspace	Deletes the character to the left of the cursor

MOUSE OPERATIONS

To *move* your mouse is to move it without pressing any buttons.

To *select* or *click* is to press the left button and immediately release it without moving the mouse. For example you click on a button to perform some operation.

CLICK
Press the left mouse button.

To *double click* is to press and release the left button twice in rapid succession without moving the mouse.

To *drag* is to press the left button and hold it as you move the mouse. You then release the button to complete the operation. In doing so you invariably *highlight* a piece of text.

DRAG
Press the left mouse button and then move the mouse.

CURSOR MOVEMENT USING THE MOUSE

The ruler can be selected from the View menu.

Pull-down menus.

Double clicking will select a single word. **Treble clicking** will select a paragraph.

Toolbars - see Appendix 1.

Clicking to the left of a line when the pointer appears will select the whole line for formatting.

Scroll up by **clicking** here.

Vertical scroll bar - **drag** to scroll the screen.

Scroll down by **clicking** here.

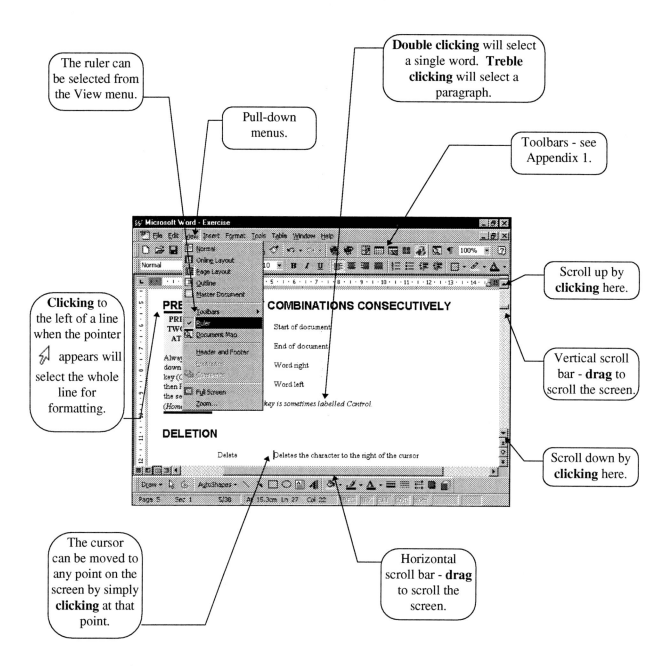

The cursor can be moved to any point on the screen by simply **clicking** at that point.

Horizontal scroll bar - **drag** to scroll the screen.

by Paul Summers

BASIC CURSOR AND POINTER TYPES

TEXT ENTRY CURSOR

The single-vertical line cursor | indicates the position in the document at which text can be entered.

TEXT CURSOR
The single-vertical line cursor | indicates the position in the document at which text can be |

THE I-BEAM POINTER

The I-beam pointer ⟂ appears where you point the mouse in the central text area of your document. **Clicking** with the I-beam pointer will change the position of the text entry cursor to the point selected. **Dragging** with the I-beam pointer will select a block of text.

THE LEFT ARROW POINTER

The left arrow pointer ⟍ appears when you point the mouse to the left of the text. **Clicking** the mouse at this stage will select/highlight the row of text to the right of the arrow. Clicking and **dragging** will highlight several lines of text. The text can then be deleted, copied, moved, made bold or italic, etc.

The left arrow pointer ⟍ appears when you point the mouse to the left of the text. **Clicking** the mouse at this stage will select/highlight the row of text to the right of the arrow. Clicking and **dragging** will highlight several lines of text. The text can then be deleted, copied, moved, made bold or italic, etc.

THE RIGHT ARROW POINTER

The right arrow pointer ⟍ appears when you point the mouse to any area of the screen where you can select a command. This could be on the pull-down menu, the buttons on the toolbar, the ruler, or the vertical and horizontal scroll bars.

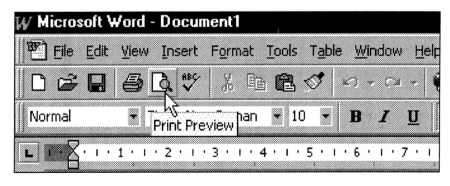

ADVANCED POINTER TYPES

DOWN ARROW POINTER

When using Tables you can quickly select an entire column for editing by clicking when the down arrow pointer appears.

A complete row can be selected simply with the left arrow pointer as detailed on the previous page.

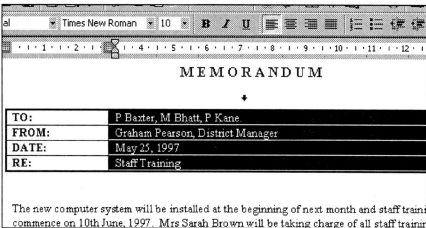

DOUBLE LINE DOUBLE ARROW

When the double line double arrow pointer appears, in tables, it can be used to adjust the widths of adjacent columns.

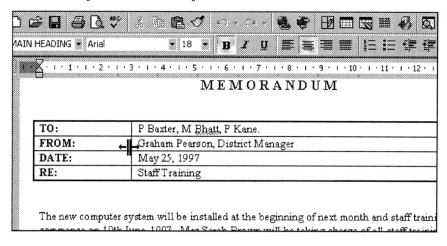

by Paul Summers

THE RULER

SWITCHING THE RULER ON/OFF

SWITCHING THE RULER ON/OFF
Select **View** and then tick ☑ **Ruler**

CHANGING THE MEASURING SYSTEM

CHANGING THE SETTING FROM INCHES TO CENTIMETERS
Select **Tools**, **Options**, **General**, Measuring units **Centimeters** and then **OK**

CHANGING THE SETTING FROM CENTIMETERS TO INCHES
Select **Tools**, **Options**, **General**, Measuring units **Inches** and then **OK**

INDENTING TEXT WITH THE RULER
The ruler can be used to change the left or right indent setting of a paragraph of text. Dragging the **First Line Indent** marker will result in the first line of the text indented.

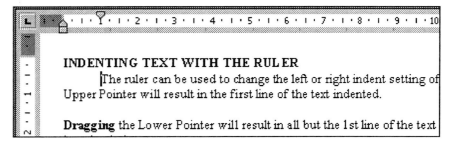

Dragging the **Hanging Indent** marker will result in all but the 1st line of the text being indented.

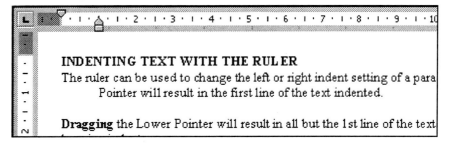

Dragging the **Left Indent** box will result in the entire paragraph being indented. The right indent can be adjusted by dragging the **Right Indent** marker.

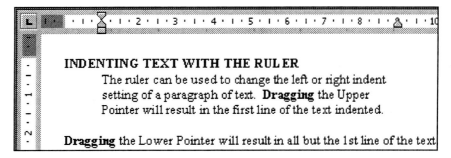

SETTING TABS ON THE RULER

Tabs can be set by simply clicking at the appropriate point on the ruler. The type of tab, **Left Tab** , **Right Tab** , **Center Tab** , or **Decimal Tab** can be set by clicking on the Tab Selection Box to the left of the ruler.

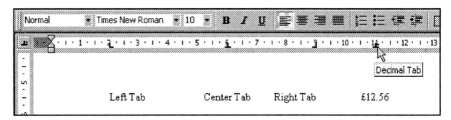

ADJUSTING MARGINS

The left and right and top and bottom margins of a document can be adjusted by **dragging** them when the double arrow, either ◄─► or ↕ appears.

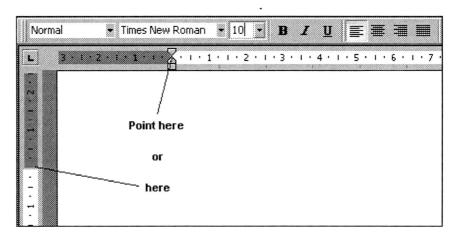

USING THESE EXERCISES

These exercises have all been written on the assumption that your screen setup is as follows:

♦ The ruler is ON
Select **View** and tick ☑ **Ruler** to switch on
♦ The ruler is set to CENTIMETERS
Select **Tools**, **Options**, **General**, select the Measuring units **Centimeters** and then **OK**
♦ Page Layout View is selected in the View menu
Select **View** and then **Page Layout**
♦ The Automatic spell checking facility is ON
Select **Tools**, **Options**, **Spelling & Grammar**, tick ☑ the **Check spelling as you type** box, and then click **OK**

Failure to set the above at the start of each lesson could result in difficulty in some of the exercises in this workbook so it is advisable to check the above before starting each lesson.

by Paul Summers

EXERCISE 1

OBJECTIVES

♦ To write a standard business letter informing a customer of a delay due to unforeseen demand.

INSTRUCTIONS

1. Open a new document.

> *OPENING A NEW DOCUMENT*
> Select **File**, **New**, choose the **General** tab, highlight the **Blank Document**, select to Create new **Document**, and then **OK**

2. Type the letter as it appears over the page. To right align the address, date and reference use the **Align Right** 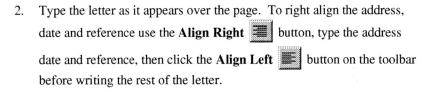 button, type the address date and reference, then click the **Align Left** 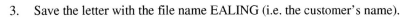 button on the toolbar before writing the rest of the letter.

3. Save the letter with the file name EALING (i.e. the customer's name).

> *SAVING A LETTER*
> Select **File** and then **Save**
> Click in the **File name** box and then enter the name of
> your document as **EALING**
> Select to Save in the **3 ½ Floppy (A:)** folder
> Click the **Save** button

4. Print preview the letter before printing.

> *PRINT PREVIEW*
> Click the **Print Preview** button on the toolbar
> Click **Close** when you have finished

5. Print the letter.

> *PRINTING A LETTER*
> Click the **Print** button on the toolbar

6. Clear the screen by selecting **File** and then **Close**.

The Furniture Company
190/196 The High Street
Willesden
London
NW10 3XD
Tel: 0181 459 0011

18/04/97
Our Ref: PB/ACH

Ealing Furniture Ltd
11 Broadway Buildings
Boston Road
London
W7

Dear Mr Kane

YOUR ORDER - CARPENTER'S WALL CLOCK

Thank you for your recent order for 20 Carpenter's Wall Clocks, Stock Code 256/1712 @£56.99 each, which we received today. We regret that due to unforeseen demand for the above named item we are currently out of stock. We have placed an order with our suppliers and they will deliver late next week. We will despatch the items to you immediately they arrive.

We trust that this delay will not inconvenience you and we look forward to your custom in the future.

Yours sincerely

Mrs P Baxter
Sales Manager

by Paul Summers

EXERCISE 2

OBJECTIVES

♦ Changing fonts, font size and case.

♦ Inserting a Text Box and then a picture/logo.

INSTRUCTIONS

1. Open the letter called EALING as written in Exercise 1.

OPEN AN EXISTING DOCUMENT
Click the **Open** 📂 document button on the toolbar
Highlight the **3 ½ Floppy (A:)** folder in the Look in box
Type **EALING** in the File name box
Click to **Open** the file

2. To read about Formatting Paragraphs click **Help**; **Contents and Index**; **Index**; type **Paragraphs** and then click to **Display** the topics available. Select a topic and then click to **Display** it. Read the various Word Help topics and then close the Word Help window by clicking the **Close** ☒ Window button.

3. Change the company name "The Furniture Company" to a different font and different size.

CHANGING FONT AND FONT SIZE
Highlight **The Furniture Company** at the top of the address by **dragging** the pointer across it
Click on the Font box and highlight **Arial**
Click on the Font Size box and highlight **22**

Click the **Bold** 🅱 button on the toolbar

Click the **Align Left** button on the toolbar

4.   Change the company name to uppercase (capital) letters.

> *CHANGING CASE*
> Highlight **The Furniture Company**
> Select **Format, Change Case, UPPERCASE** and **OK**
> **Click** at the start of the line *190/196 The High Street* to deselect
> the highlighting of *The Furniture Company*

5.   To read about Graphics and Text Boxes click **Help**; **Contents and
     Index**; **Contents**; *double-click* **Importing Graphics and Creating
     Drawing Objects**; *double-click* **Positioning Text and Graphics**;
     double-click **About positioning text and graphics**. Read the various
     Word Help topics and then close the Word Help window by clicking the
     Close ☒ Window button.

6.   Place a Text Box in the top right hand corner of the document.

> *PLACING A TEXT BOX ON THE PAGE*
> Select **Insert** and then **Text Box**
> Draw a small box to the right of THE FURNITURE COMPANY
> as shown below by clicking and **dragging** the mouse from the top
> left to the bottom right corner
> **Click** on the outline of the box so that the 8 small boxes (handles)
> appear around the Text Box as shown

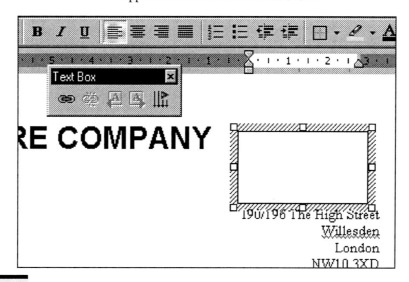

7.   Format the Text Box to fit in the top right hand corner of the document
     (in-line with the document margins) and to accept a picture with
     dimensions 1.6cm by 2.5cm.

> *FORMATTING A TEXT BOX*
> Select **Format** and **Text Box**
> *REMOVE THE BORDER LINE AROUND THE TEXT BOX*
> Choose the **Colors and Lines** tab
> Select Line Color **No Line**
> N.B. *The Text Box itself will now appear invisible.*

by Paul Summers

SET THE SIZE OF THE TEXT BOX
Choose the **Size** tab
Set the Height as **1.6 cm**
Set the Width as **2.5 cm**
SET THE POSITION OF THE TEXT BOX
Choose the **Position** tab
Set the Horizontal position **12 cm** From the *left* **Margin**
Set the Vertical position **0 cm** From the *top* **Margin**
Select **Lock Anchor** by placing a tick ☑ in the box
SET THE WRAPPING OF THE TEXT BOX
Choose the **Wrapping** tab
Set the Wrapping style to **Square**
Set the Wrap to **Left**
N.B. *Text will remain to the left and below the Text Box.*
SET THE INTERNAL MARGINS OF THE TEXT BOX
Choose the **Text Box** tab
Set the Internal margin Left to **0 cm**
Set the Internal margin Right to **0 cm**
Set the Internal margin Top to **0 cm**
Set the Internal margin Bottom to **0 cm**
N.B. *The picture will now fill out the Text Box.*
ACCEPTING THE SETTINGS
Finally click **OK** to save the changes

8. Place a picture/logo in the Text Box.

   PLACING A PICTURE/LOGO INSIDE A TEXT BOX
   Click inside the Text Box
   Select **Insert, Picture** and then **From File**
   Select to Look in **3 ½ Floppy (A:)** folder
   type **REAL ESTATE** in the File name box, then click **OK**
   ADJUSTING THE ADDRESS
   Move the address of the company down below the picture if
   necessary by placing the cursor in front of "190/196 The High
   Street" and pressing **Enter** as many times as necessary

9. Save the letter with the existing file name EALING.

   SAVING AN EXISTING LETTER
   Click the **Save** 🖫 button on the toolbar

10. **Print Preview** 🔍 and **Print** 🖨 the document.

11. Clear the screen by selecting **File** and then **Close**.

THE FURNITURE COMPANY

190/196 The High Street
Willesden
London
NW10 3XD
Tel: 0181 459 0011

18/04/97
Our Ref: PB/ACH

Ealing Furniture Ltd
11 Broadway Buildings
Boston Road
London
W7

Dear Mr Kane

YOUR ORDER - CARPENTER'S WALL CLOCK

Thank you for your recent order for 20 Carpenter's Wall Clocks, Stock Code 256/1712 @ £56.99 each, which we received today. We regret that due to unforeseen demand for the above named item we are currently out of stock. We have placed an order with our suppliers and they will deliver late next week. We will despatch the items to you immediately they arrive.

We trust that this delay will not inconvenience you and we look forward to your custom in the future.

Yours sincerely

Mrs P Baxter
Sales Manager

EXERCISE 3

OBJECTIVES

♦ Writing a business letter informing a candidate that she has not been successful in applying for a job.

♦ Creating the company header, including logo, as part of the letter.

♦ Changing the Margins.

♦ Using Protected Space.

INSTRUCTIONS

1. Open a new document.

    OPENING A NEW DOCUMENT
    Click the **New** document button on the toolbar

2. Change the top and bottom margins.

    CHANGING MARGINS
    Select **File**, **Page Setup**, choose the **Margins** tab, type **4 cm** as the Top margin, type **4 cm** as the Bottom margin, then click **OK**

3. Type the content of the letter as it appears over the page entering the company name in ordinary text first. Follow the instructions over the page to protect the spaces in the phrase *The Furniture Company*. Do NOT included the picture/logo just yet.

4. Save the letter with the file name JOHNSON.

    SAVING A LETTER
    Select **File** and then **Save**
    Click in the **File name** box and then enter the name of your document as **JOHNSON**
    Select to Save in the **3 ½ Floppy (A:)** folder
    Click the **Save** button

5. Repeat the instructions in Exercise 2 previous to place the company name and logo at the top of the page.

6. **Save** the corrected document.

7. **Print Preview** and **Print** the document.

8. **Close** the document.

CLOSE

A quick way to close the document is to **click** on the document control button in the *upper right corner* of the document window. Take care NOT to close Word 97.

THE FURNITURE COMPANY

190/196 The High Street
Willesden
London
NW10 3XD
Tel: 0181 459 0011

7 June 1997
Our Ref: PW/ACH

Ms Johnson
10 Park Road
Harlesden
London
NW10 3QP

Dear Ms Johnson,

YOUR INQUIRY CONCERNING POSSIBLE EMPLOYMENT

Thank you for your inquiry about employment opportunities at The Furniture Company.
The Furniture Company appreciate your interest in employment with the company.

Although your background is impressive, we currently have no openings that match your skills and qualifications. We will keep your details on file for one year for review should we have an opening for which you are qualified.

Again, thank you for your interest. Best wishes for success in your career search.

Yours sincerely,

```
    PROTECTED SPACE

Hold down both the Shift and Ctrl
keys and press the Spacebar between
The and Furniture and between
Furniture and Company to hold the
three words together.
```

Mr P Wilson
Human Resources Manager

by Paul Summers

EXERCISE 4

OBJECTIVES

♦ Writing a business letter informing a customer that you are dealing with their complaint about damaged goods.

♦ Correcting the letter to include the company house style, a reference line, an attention line and the company heading and logo.

♦ Setting margins.

INSTRUCTIONS

1. Open a **New** 🗋 document.

2. Change the top and bottom margins.

   CHANGING MARGINS
   Select **File**, **Page Setup**, choose the **Margins** tab, type **4 cm** as the Top margin, type **4 cm** as the Bottom margin, then click **OK**

3. Type the letter as it appears over the page.

4. Save the letter with the file name LEE.

   SAVING A LETTER
   Select **File** and **Save**
   Click in the **File name** box and enter the name of your document as **LEE**
   Select to Save in the **3 ½ Floppy (A:)** folder
   Click to **Save** the file on your disc

5. The letter does not conform to the standards of the letters produced in Exercises 2 and 3. Modify the letter by:

   aligning right the company address,
   including a reference line (initials of the person the letter is from and who types it),
   including an attention line (what the letter is about),
   including the company heading and logo.

6. **Save** 🖫 the corrected document.

7. **Print Preview** 🔍 and **Print** 🖨 the document.

8. **Close** ✖ the document.

SAVE OFTEN

A quick way to save a document is to click the **Save** button on the toolbar. With documents that take a long time to write it is advisable to save regularly, say every 5 to 10 minutes.

Insert company name and logo.

190/196 The High Street
Willesden
London
NW10 3XD
Tel: 0181 459 0011

7 June 1997

Reference line goes here. You decide what to put.

Mr P Lee
108 Craven Park Road
Harlesden
London
NW10 8QD

Attention Line goes here. You decide what to write.

Dear Mr Lee,

Your 6 May 1997 letter regarding the delivery of damaged merchandise was forwarded to me. I am looking into the situation and I hope to resolve it quickly. When I have finished my investigation, I will write or call you with a response.

I assure you that we are taking your complaint very seriously. You are a valuable customer, and any dissatisfaction on your part indicates an opportunity for improvement on our part.

If I need more information from you to help me resolve this matter, I will contact you. Thank you for your patience.

Yours sincerely,

Ms M Bhatt
Account Representative

EXERCISE 5

OBJECTIVES

♦ Use the Spelling checker to check a document.

INSTRUCTIONS

1. **Open** the document **SPELLING** from your disc.

2. To read about Spell Checking click **Help**; **Contents and Index**; **Index**; type **Spell Checking** and then click to **Display** the topics available. Select a topic and then click to **Display** it. Read the various Word Help topics and then close the Word Help window by clicking the **Close** ⊠ Window button.

3. Use the spell checker.

AUTOMATIC SPELL CHECKING

Word 97 underlines words which are spelt wrong if the "Check spelling as you type" option is selected in the Options menu.

STARTING THE SPELL CHECKER
Place the cursor at the *start* of the document
Click the **Spelling** [abc] button on the toolbar
CORRECTING OR IGNORING ERRORS
Copany is spelt incorrectly click on **Change** to correct it
Willesden is spelt correctly click on **Add** to add it to the dictionary
Harlesden is spelt correctly click on **Add** to add it to the dictionary
Leter is spelt incorrectly click on **Change** to correct it
Leter is spelt incorrectly click on **Change** to correct it
CORRECTING MORE COMPLICATED ERRORS
Pussable is spelt incorrectly and although the dictionary list includes the answer you must highlight it first, click on **possible** in the Suggestions box, then click on **Change**

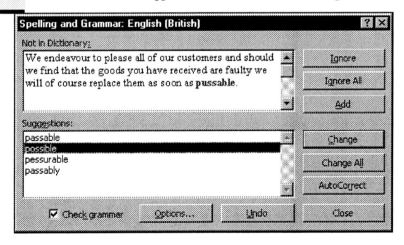

Funitue is spelt incorrectly and this time the dictionary does not list it, edit *funitue* to read **furniture**, then click **Change**
Finally select **OK** to finish spell checking

4.   The spell checker does not always work.

   PROOF READING
   The line *Re: Your letter dated 17th May 1997 - faulty gods.*
   should read **faulty goods** correct it

5.   **Save** ▣ the corrected document.

6.   **Print Preview** ▣ and **Print** ▣ the document.

7.   **Close** ▣ the document.

by Paul Summers

Text to be corrected by the spell checker is in bold and italic.

The Furniture *Copany*
190/196 The High Street
Willesden
London
NW10 3XD
Tel: 0181 459 0011

7 June 1997
Ref: PK/ACH

Ms S.C. Turner
12a Manor Park Road
Harlesden
London
NW10 4XD

Dear Ms Turner,

Re: Your *leter* dated 17th May 1997 - faulty *gods*.

Thank you for your *leter* of the 17th of May concerning the table and 4 chairs you purchased from us recently. I am sorry to hear that you have had problems assembling 2 of the chairs. I am not quite clear from your letter as exactly what the problem is and as such would be grateful if you could phone me with further details or alternatively come to our showroom and speak to me personally.

We endeavour to please all of our customers and should we find that the goods you have received are faulty we will of course replace them as soon as *pussable*. If that is not to your satisfaction then you can of course claim a refund for the complete set of *funitue* you purchased.

I look forward to hearing from you soon.

Yours sincerely,

Peter Kane
Sales Manager

EXERCISE 6

OBJECTIVES

♦ Correcting a business letter. (See Proof Correction Symbols - Appendix 2).

♦ Changing the main font from Times New Roman (a proportional font) to Courier New (a non-proportional font).

INSTRUCTIONS

1. **Open** [icon] the document **JENNINGS**.

2. Make the necessary corrections to the document as shown over the page.

PROPORTIONAL AND NON-PROPORTIONAL FONTS

Times New Roman gives more space to wider characters and less space to narrower characters.

Courier New gives the same space to all characters.

---

3. Click on the **Spelling** [icon] button to check the document.

4. **Save** [icon] the corrected document.

5. **Print Preview** [icon] and **Print** [icon] the document.

6. Change to a non-proportional font.

NON-PROPORTIONAL FONT
Select **Edit** and **Select All**
Select **Courier New** (a non-proportional font) in the font box

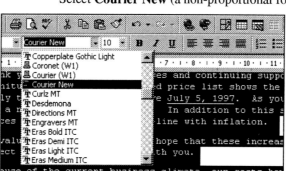

7. **Save** [icon] the corrected document.

8. **Print Preview** [icon] and **Print** [icon] the document.

9. **Close** [icon] the document.

THE FURNITURE COMPANY

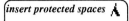

insert protected spaces

190/196 The High Street
Willesden
London
NW10 3XD
Tel: 0181 459 0011

7 June 1997

Our Ref: AJ/ACH

Jennings House Furnishers
54 Shenley Road
Borehamwood
Herts
WD6 2AS

Dear mr Jennings,

Re: New catalogue including a number of special ~~SALE~~ offers.

insert protected spaces

Thank you for your past purchases and continuing support of The Furniture Company. The enclosed price list shows the prices that apply to all purchases effective July 5, 1997. As you can see, there are a number of special offers. In addition to this some of our prices have had to increase in-line with inflation.

We value you as a customer and hope that these increases will not affect our good relationship with you.

Because of the current business climate, our costs have increased. We can no longer ~~longer~~ maintain all of our prices at their past levels and still continue to provide the superior quality and service that you have come to expect from us.

Yours sincerely,

Alan Jones
Accounts Representative

EXERCISE 7

OBJECTIVES

♦ Correcting a business letter.

♦ Changing the main font from Times New Roman (a proportional font) to Courier New (a non-proportional font) for part of the letter.

♦ Using a Superscript to add a footnote to a document.

INSTRUCTIONS

1. **Open** ⬛ the document **ASCOT**.

2. Make the necessary corrections to the document as shown over the page.

3. Click on the **Spelling** ⬛ button to check the document. There should be 2 errors to correct *manufacturer* and *fault.*

4. **Save** ⬛ the corrected document.

5. **Print Preview** ⬛ and **Print** ⬛ the document.

6. Change part of the letter to a non-proportional font.

   NON-PROPORTIONAL FONT
   Highlight the text from **190/196 The High Street** down to
   Purchasing Manager at the bottom of the letter
   Select **Courier New** (a non-proportional font) in the font box
   N.B. *The heading will still remain in Arial font which is a proportional font type.*

7. Use a superscript to add a footnote (see Exercise 26 for an alternative way to add a footnote).

   USING A SUPERSCRIPT
   Place the cursor at the end of *Rectangular drop kitchen table*
   Select **Format, Font,** tick ☑ the **Superscript** box, click **OK**
   Type the number **1** which will appear small and above the line
   Select **Format, Font,** remove the tick ☐ from the **Superscript** box, then click **OK**
   At the very bottom of the letter below *Mr P Newman* type
   [1] **We will re-order this at a future date.**

8. **Save** 🖫 the corrected document.

9. **Print Preview** 🔍 and **Print** 🖨 the document.

10. **Close** ✖ the document.

THE ᴧFURNITURE ᴧCOMPANY

insert protected spaces ᴧ

190/196 The High Street
Willesden
London
NW10
Tel: 0181 459 0011

7 June 1997
Our Ref: PN/ACH

Ascot Furnishing Fabrics Ltd
16 Fimer Road
Fulham
London
SW6 1AG
Tel: 0181 385 1612

Re: Order number 1003.

Dear John,

Please cancel our order number 1003, dated May 6, 1997, for:

make underline

make bold

Item Code	Description	Qty
600/2057	Rectangular drop kitchen table[1]	100
600/ ᴧ2840	Kitchen chairs	400

2480 ᴧ

0.5"

We regret that we are unable to wait for the delayed shipment from the manufcturer.

We understand that this delay was not your faut. We will keep in mind you for similar requirements that we may have in the future.

Yours sincerely,

Mr P Newman
ᴧ

ᴧ*Purchasing Manager*

---

[1] We will order this at a future date.

by Paul Summers

EXERCISE 8

OBJECTIVES

♦ Correcting the company pension scheme document.

♦ Using the Replace command.

INSTRUCTIONS

1. **Open** 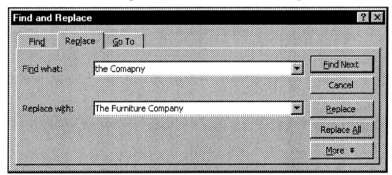 the document **PENSION**.

2. Make the necessary corrections to the document as shown over the page.

3. Click on the **Spelling** button to check the document.

4. To read about Replacing Text click **Help**; **Contents and Index**; **Contents**; *double-click* **Editing and Sorting**; *double-click* **Finding and Replacing Text and Formatting**; *double-click* **Find and replace**. Select one of the What do you want to do? topics to display it. Read the various Word Help topics and then close the Word Help window by clicking the **Close** Window button.

5. Use the Replace command to change *the Company* to *The Furniture Company*.

   USING REPLACE
   Select **Edit**, **Replace**, type **the Company** in the Find what box, type **The Furniture Company** (use protected spaces) in the Replace with box, then click to **Replace All**

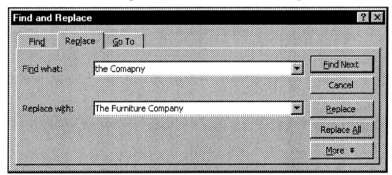

6. **Save** the corrected document.

7. **Print Preview** and **Print** the document.

8. Select **Edit** and then **Select All**, then change all of the letter to a non-proportional font such as **Courier New** (see previous exercise).

9. **Save** ▣ the corrected document.

10. **Print Preview** ▣ and **Print** ▣ the document.

11. **Close** ▣ the document.

THE FURNITURE COMPANY'S PENSION FUND _Make the heading bold/underlined/centred/12pt_

The amount of pension to be drawn by you when you retire will depend upon a number of factors. These include the number of years of service given by you to The Furniture Company, the contributions you make, as well as the average salary that you are on for the final 5 years of service to the ∧Company. Further details are ∧attached showing your current position with regards to:

∧Furniture

∧available on request

∧Furniture

(i)   the ammount of pension to be credited in respect of years of service to the ∧Company;

_0.5"_

(ii)   your annual contributions to date plus predicted contributions for the future; and,

(iii) details of your salary for the last 5 years and the contribution this would make to your pension.

Should you decide to leave the service of the Company before retirment, all contributions which you will have made towards this Scheme will be refunded to you with appropriate provision for inflasion which is calculated in-line with the Government's figure for pensions of 3% per annum. In other words, if you do not reach retirement age with us, your contributions can be considered as a form of saving. Should wish you to transfer the contributions made to another pension scheme that can be arranged with you new employer and/or a private pension provider.

_3.5%_

The pension will be paid for as long as you live, but if you do not receive from us a pension for 3 years or more after retiring the pension will continue to be paid to your ∧dependents so long as ∧they shall live.

∧husband/wife

∧he/she

_£5000_

With your contributions to date you are entitled to an annual pension of £6000 when you reach retirement age (65 yrs for men and 60 yrs for ladies). Based upon your present salary grade your continued contribution has been calculated at £20.00 per week. This will be deducted directly from your salary on a monthly basis averaged over the year. Income Tax Relief will be deducted from your contributions at the appropriate rate. An additional contribution payable by The Furniture Company will be made which will be the equivalent of 110% of your contribution. At present this stands at £22.00 per week.

EXERCISE 9

OBJECTIVES

♦ To write a letter using AutoText.

INSTRUCTIONS

1. **Open** 📂 the document called **JENNINGS**.

2. Create two pieces of AutoText.

    CREATING AUTOTEXT
    Place the cursor at the *start* of the document
    Drag the pointer across the text from **THE FURNITURE COMPANY** to the end of the reference line **Our Ref: AJ/ACH**
    Select **Insert, AutoText, New**, type the name of your AutoText entry **COMPANY**, then click **OK**

    Scroll down the page to where it says *Yours sincerely*
    Drag the pointer across the text from **Yours sincerely** to **Account Representative** at the end of the document
    Select **Insert, AutoText, New**, type the name of your AutoText entry **AlanJones**, then click **OK**

3. Click the **New** ▢ document button on the toolbar to open a new document.

4. Insert AutoText into a new document.

    INSERTING AUTOTEXT
    Select **Insert**, **AutoText**, and then **AutoText** again
    Highlight **COMPANY** in the Enter AutoText entries box
    Click the **Insert** button

5. Type the text of the letter shown over the page from **Dear Mr Wilson** down to **...... the next few days**.

6. Insert AutoText into a new document.

    INSERTING AUTOTEXT
    Select **Insert**, **AutoText**, and then **AutoText** again
    Highlight **AlanJones** in the Enter AutoText entries box
    Click the **Insert** button

7. **Save** [icon] the file with the File name **WILSON** (i.e. the customers name).

8. **Print Preview** [icon] and **Print** [icon] the document.

9. **Close** [icon] both documents.

AutoText

Using AutoText with graphic images does not always work.

THE FURNITURE COMPANY

190/196 The High Street
Willesden
London
NW10 3XD
Tel: 0181 459 0011

7 June 1997
Our Ref: AJ/ACH

Dear Mr Wilson

Thank you for your prompt response to my letter of the 24th of May. I am dealing with the matter as a matter of some urgency and will be in contact with you within the next few days.

Yours sincerely,

Alan Jones
Account Representative

EXERCISE 10

OBJECTIVES

♦ To create a letter Template.

INSTRUCTIONS

1. Create a new Template.

   OPENING A TEMPLATE
   Select **File**, **New**, select the **General** tab, highlight the **Blank Document** option, select to Create New **Template**, then click **OK**

2. Set the Top and Bottom margins to **4 cm** (as in Exercise 4).

3. Type in the letter as it appears over the page. This is an outline/template for a range of letters Mrs Baxter could write.

4. Save the template.

   SAVING THE TEMPLATE
   Select **File** and then **Save**
   Click in the **File name** box and type *YOUR NAME* **TEMPLATE**
   N.B. *It must say Document Template in the Save as type box.*
   Select to Save in the **Templates** folder *on the hard disc*
   N.B. *If you get an error message it is probably because the system is protected and does not allow you to save to it.*
   Click the **Save** button

5. **Close** ☒ the document.

6. Open a new document based on the Template.

   USING A TEMPLATE
   Select **File**, **New**, select the **General** tab, highlight *YOUR NAME* **TEMPLATE**, select to Create New **Document**, then click **OK**

7. Type the following message to Mr Kane.

SAVING TEMPLATES

If the hard disc or file server is write protected you will NOT be able to save your template there.

It is possible to Save the template on the a:\ drive. Select **Tools**, **Options**, **File Locations**, highlight **User Templates** and click the **Modify** button, select to Look in the **3 ½ Floppy (A:)** folder, then click **OK** and then **Close**. This may only work temporarily depending on the system setup.

Dear Mr Kane

YOUR ORDER - CARPENTER'S WALL CLOCK

Further to our letter of the 18th of May we are pleased to inform you that your order for 20 Carpenter's Wall Clocks, Stock Code 256/1712 @ £56.99, will be dispatched to you today.

We trust that this delay did not inconvenience you and we look forward to your custom in the future.

8. **Save** the letter with the File name **KANE**. N.B. *The original Template will not be affected when you save this document, it will still be blank. Repeat 6 above and see.*

9. **Print Preview** and **Print** the document.

10. **Close** the document.

The Furniture Company
190/196 The High Street
Willesden
London
NW10 3XD
Tel: 0181 459 0011

11/05/97
Our Ref: PB/ACH

Dear

Yours sincerely

Mrs P Baxter
Sales Manager

EXERCISE 11

OBJECTIVES

♦   Writing a standard business letter using Letter Wizard.

INSTRUCTIONS

1.   Create a standard letter using the Letter Wizard.

USING LETTER WIZARD
Select **File, New**, choose the **Letters & Faxes** tab, highlight
Letter Wizard, select to Create New **Document**, then click **OK**
Select to **Send one letter** and then click **OK**
Tick ☑ to include a **Date line**, Choose the page design
Contemporary Letter, then click **Next**
Type the Recipient's name as **ALL OUR CUSTOMERS**,
select a Salutation **Informal**, then click **Next**
Choose to Include an ☑ **Attention line**, type the attention line
entry **NEW PRICE LIST**, then click **Next**
Type the Sender's name **Alan Jones**, the Return address as
    190/196 The High Street
    Willesden
    London NW10 3XD
    Tel: 0181 459 0011
Choose the Complementary closing remark **Yours sincerely**,
type the Job title **Accounts Representative**, then click **Finish**

2.   Make the corrections to the standard computer generated letter as shown over the page.

3.   **Save** 🖫 the letter with the File name **ALL CUSTOMERS**.

4.   **Print Preview** 🔍 and **Print** 🖨 the document.

5.   **Close** ✖ the document.

by Paul Summers

◆
◆
◆
◆
◆

190/196 The High Street
Willesden
London NW10 3XD
Tel: 0181 459 0011

09 July 1997

ALL OUR CUSTOMERS

NEW PRICE LIST

Dear ALL,

Thank you for your past purchases and continuing support of The Furniture Company. The enclosed
price list shows the prices that apply to all purchases effective 5 July 1997. As you can see, there have
been some price increases.

Because of the current business climate, our costs have increased. We can no longer maintain all of our
prices at their past levels and still continue to provide the superior quality and service that you have
come to expect from us.

We value you as a customer and hope that these increases will not affect our good relationship with
you.

Yours sincerely

Alan Jones
Accounts Representative

◆ ◆ ◆ ◆ ◆ ◆ ◆ ◆ ◆ ◆ ◆ ◆ ◆ ◆ ◆ ◆ ◆ ◆ ◆ ◆

EXERCISE 12

OBJECTIVES

♦ Writing a standard business Memo.

INSTRUCTIONS

1. Open a **New** ▯ document.

2. Enter the text as shown over the page to include:

   a) the company heading and logo,
   b) the heading **M E M O R A N D U M** in bold, centred, with Font size 12pt, and with spaces between each character,
   c) the headings **TO:**, **FROM:**, **DATE:** and **RE:** in uppercase and bold.

3. **Save** ▯ the letter with the File name **MEMO Staff Training**.

4. **Print Preview** ▯ and **Print** ▯ the document.

5. **Close** ▯ the document.

THE FURNITURE COMPANY

M E M O R A N D U M

TO: P Baxter, M Bhatt, P Kane.

FROM: Graham Pearson, District Manager

DATE: May 25, 1997

RE: Staff Training

The new computer system will be installed at the beginning of next month and staff training will commence on 10th June, 1997. Mrs Sarah Brown will be taking charge of all staff training from that date.

I have spoken to Mrs Brown and she would like to start the training program with the managers. She will then begin the secretaries training in the second week.

Mrs Brown has had a great deal of experience in these matters and I hope that everyone will co-operate with her wishes. She feels that a three week training period should be sufficient to cover the transition from our manual to the computerised system.

EXERCISE 13

OBJECTIVES

♦ Enhancing a standard business memo by adding a Table.

INSTRUCTIONS

1. **Open** 🖻 the document **MEMO Staff Training**.

2. Delete the section of the memo from **TO:** down to **RE: Staff Training**.

3. To read about Tables click **Help**; **Contents and Index**; **Contents**; *double-click* **Working with Tables and Adding Borders**; *double-click* **About working with tables**. Read the various Word Help topics and then close the Word Help window by clicking the **Close** 🗙 Window button.

4. Create a table.

   CREATING A TABLE
   Place the cursor in a blank line between *MEMORANDUM* and *The new computer system ....*
   Select **Table**, **Insert Table**, select the Number of columns as **2**, the Number of rows as **4**, then click **OK**
   Adjust the width of the columns by **dragging** the centre line, when the ◄▐► appears, across to the 3 cm mark on the ruler

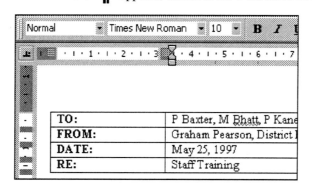

5. Type in the details of the who the memo is To, From, etc.

6. Select **File** and then **Save As** to save the letter with the File name **MEMO Staff Training Update**.

7. **Print Preview** 🔍 and **Print** 🖨 the document.

8. **Close** 🗙 the document.

by Paul Summers

THE FURNITURE COMPANY

MEMORANDUM

TO:	P Baxter, M Bhatt, P Kane.
FROM:	Graham Pearson, District Manager
DATE:	May 25, 1997
RE:	Staff Training

The new computer system will be installed at the beginning of next month and staff training will commence on 10th June, 1997. Mrs Sarah Brown will be taking charge of all staff training from that date.

I have spoken to Mrs Brown and she would like to start the training program with the managers. She will then begin the secretaries training in the second week.

Mrs Brown has had a great deal of experience in these matters and I hope that everyone will co-operate with her wishes. She feels that a three week training period should be sufficient to cover the transition from our manual to the computerised system.

EXERCISE 14

OBJECTIVES

♦ Writing an agenda setting memo.

♦ Using line numbering and indenting.

♦ Using a Superscript to add a footnote to a document.

INSTRUCTIONS

1. Open a **New** document.

2. Enter the text as shown over the page. Use a Table, as in Exercise 13.

3. Create the numbered list of agenda topics.

> *LINE NUMBERING*
> Type in the 5 topics on the agenda with NO blank lines between them
> Highlight the 5 topics by **dragging** the pointer across them
> Click the line **Numbering** button on the toolbar
> Click the **Increase Indent** button on the toolbar *three times*
> Place the cursor at the end of each successive line and hold down the **Shift** key and press **Enter** to add the blank lines

SUBSCRIPT

Repeat part 4 this time selecting Subscript instead of Superscript. Subscript text appears below the line. Superscript text appears above the line.

4. Use a superscript to add a footnote.

> *USING A SUPERSCRIPT*
> Place the cursor at the end of *Minutes of previous meeting*.
> Select **Format, Font,** choose the **Font** tab, tick ☑ the Effects **Superscript** box and then **OK**, type the number **1** which will appear small and above the line, select **Format, Font,** choose the **Font** tab, remove the tick from the **Superscript** box, and then click **OK**
> At the very bottom of the document type
> [1] **The minutes will be available in the next few days.**

5. Repeat 4 above to place footnote number 2 as shown over the page.

6. **Save** the letter with the File name **AGENDA**.

7. **Print Preview** and **Print** the document.

8. **Close** the document.

THE FURNITURE COMPANY

M E M O R A N D U M

TO:	Ms S O'Connor, Mr T Bendon, Miss R Green, Mr P Bowman.
FROM:	Graham Pearson, District Manager
DATE:	Friday 19th May 1997 at 1500 hrs, Conference Room.
RE:	Weekly status meeting of the Senior Management Committee.

There will be a short meeting of the senior Management Committee this Friday. The Agenda for the meeting is as follows:

1. Minutes of previous meeting.[1]

2. Weekly sales figures.

3. Details of staff training day.[2]

4. Responsibilities on stock taking day.

5. Any other business.

[1] The minutes will be available in the next few days.
[2] Further details will be sent to you before the meeting. Please read.

EXERCISE 15

OBJECTIVES

♦   Writing up the Minutes of a meeting.

INSTRUCTIONS

1.   Open a **New** ☐ document.

2.   Enter the heading, the logo, type in the details of where the meeting was held and who was present.

3.   Create the numbered list of agenda details.

> *LINE NUMBERING*
> Type in the 8 topics from **APOLOGIES FOR ABSENCE** down to **NEXT MEETING** simply as headings - i.e. do NOT include the details yet
> Highlight the 8 topics by **dragging** the pointer across them
> Click the line **Numbering** ☰ button on the toolbar
> Place the cursor at the end of each line and hold down the **Shift** key and press **Enter** to add the blank lines
> Type in the details of each of the agenda items as shown over the page

4.   **Save** 🖫 the letter with the File name **MINUTES**.

5.   **Print Preview** 🔍 and **Print** 🖨 the document.

6.   **Close** ☒ the document.

by Paul Summers

THE FURNITURE COMPANY

MINUTES OF MEETING

A meeting of the Senior Management Committee of The Furniture Company was held on Friday 19th May 1997 at 1500 hrs.

<u>PRESENT</u>

Mr G Pearson, Ms S O'Connor, Mr T Bendon, Miss R Green.

1. APOLOGIES FOR ABSENCE

    The Secretary reported that Mr P Bowman was unable to attend as he was away on business.

2. MINUTES OF LAST MEETING

    The Minutes of the last meeting were read, approved and signed by the Chairperson.

3. MATTERS ARISING FROM MINUTES

    The Secretary reported that the coach for the Annual Works outing had been booked.

4. WEEKLY SALES FIGURES

    Tony read the report on the previous weeks sales which were encouraging in that they showed a continuing upward trend.

5. DETAILS OF STAFF TRAINING

    Graham spoke about the forthcoming Computing Training to be facilitated by Mrs Sarah Brown. A three week training period was recommended by Mrs Brown. 20 staff in all would be trained.

6. RESPONSIBILITIES ON STOCK TAKING DAY

    Tony distributed details of responsibilities for the stock taking day on Monday 29th May.

7. ANY OTHER BUSINESS

    None.

8. NEXT MEETING

    The date and time of the next meeting was fixed for 26th May 1997 at 1500 hrs.

EXERCISE 16

OBJECTIVES

♦   Creating an Agenda for a meeting.

INSTRUCTIONS

1.   Create an agenda memo for the same meeting called in Exercise 14 previous, as shown over the page.

> *MAIN HEADING*
> The text **Weekly Status Meeting** should be Font Size **20pt** and made **Bold** B
>
> *DATE/TIME/PLACE*
> The **Date/Time/Place** text should be Font Size **12pt** and made **Bold** B and **Centre** ≣
>
> *SECTION HEADING*
> The text **Agenda** should be Font Size **18pt** and made **Bold** B
>
> *AGENDA DETAILS*
> To create the agenda details section place **Left Tabs** L at **7cm** and **12cm** on the ruler
> Format the **Paragraph** to **Double** Line spacing
>
> *SECTION HEADING*
> The text **Additional Information** should be Font Size **12pt** and made **Bold** B

2.   **Save** the letter with the File name **AGENDA 19th May 97**.

3.   Try adding the company heading and logo in the appropriate places.

4.   **Save** the letter again with the File name **AGENDA 19th May 97**.

5.   **Print Preview** 🔲 and **Print** 🔲 the document.

6.   **Close** ⊠ the document.

Weekly Status Meeting

19/05/97
15:00 to 16:00
Conference Room

Meeting called by: Graham Pearson.

Attendees: Mr G Pearson, Ms S O'Connor, Mr T Bendon, Miss R Green, Mr P Bowman.

Agenda

Appologies.	Graham.	15:00-15:00
Minutes of previous meeting.	Graham.	15:00-15:05
Matters arrising from previous meeting.	Secrataries report.	15:05-15:15
Weekly sales figures.	Tony.	15:15-15:25
Staff Training.	Graham.	15:25-15:35
Stock taking day.	Tony.	15:35-15:45
AOB.	Graham.	15:45-15:55
Next Meeting.	Graham.	15:55-16:00

Additional Information

EXERCISE 17

OBJECTIVES

♦ Creating an agenda for a meeting.

INSTRUCTIONS

1. Create the agenda memo shown over the page in a similar way to the previous exercise.

2. **Save** ⊞ the memo with the File name **AGENDA 26th May 97**.

3. **Print Preview** 🔍 and **Print** 🖨 the document.

4. **Close** ✖ the document.

Senior Management Committee Meeting

26/05/97
15:00 to 15:30
Conference Room

Meeting called by: John Benson.

Attendees: ALL SENIOR MANAGEMENT

Agenda

1. Appologies.	John.		15:00-15:00
2. Minutes of last meeting.	John.		15:00-15:05
3. Matters arrising from minutes.	John.		15:05-15:15
4. Responsibilities on stock taking day.	Ann.		15:15-15:25
5. A.O.B.	John.		15:25-15:30

Additional Information

EXERCISE 18

OBJECTIVES

♦   Creating a Fax using the Fax Wizard.

INSTRUCTIONS

1.   Write a Fax to a supplier querying an order.

USING THE FAX WIZARD
Select **File**, **New**, choose the **Letters & Faxes** tab, highlight the **Fax Wizard**, select to **Create New** Document, then click **OK**
Click **Next** to go to the next screen
For Which document do you want to send? select **Just a cover sheet with a note**, then click **Next**
For Which fax program do you want to use to send your fax? select **I want to print my document ...**, then click **Next**
For Who should receive the fax? type the recipient's Name **John Ascot**, then click **Next**
For Which style do you want for your cover sheet? choose a **Professional** one, then click **Next**
For Who is the fax from? type the details shown then click **Next**, and finally **Finish** to create the cover sheet

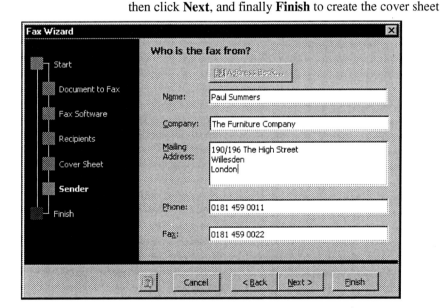

2.   Type in the rest of the Fax details as shown over the page.

3.   **Save** the document with the File name **FAX to Ascot**.

4.   **Print Preview** and **Print** the document.

5.   **Close** the document.

190/196 The High Street
Willesden
London
Phone: 0181 459 0011
Fax: 0181 459 0022

**The Furniture
Company**

FAX

To:	John Ascot	**From:**	YOUR NAME
Fax:	0134	**Date:**	April 10, 1997
Phone:	0181 385 1612	**Page:**	1
Re:	Order 23789	**CC:**	

☒ Urgent   ☐ For Review   ☐ Please Comment   ☐ Please Reply   ☐ Please Recycle

Comments:

We placed an order for 100 Black Ash Tables @ £24.99 each 10 days ago but have received no correspondence from you. Could you please investigate the matter and get back to me immediately.

by Paul Summers

EXERCISE 19

OBJECTIVES

♦ Sending memos using Mail Merge.

INSTRUCTIONS

1. **Open** 📂 the document **MEMO Staff Training Update**.

2. Delete the names of the persons the memo is addressed to in the TO: box. At the bottom of the memo press **Enter** several times and then type in **c.c. Mr P Baxter, Mr M Bhatt, Mr P Kane.**

3. Use **Save As** to save the letter with the File name **MERGE**.

4. To read about Mail Merge click **Help**; **Contents and Index**; **Contents**; *double-click* **Assembling Documents with Mail Merge**; *double-click* **Form letters, envelopes, and labels**. Read the various Word Help topics and then close the Word Help window by clicking the **Close** ⊠ Window button.

5. Use Mail Merge to address the same document to different people.

   USING MAIL MERGE
   Select **Tools** and then **Mail Merge**
   Click the **Create** a Main document button, select **Form Letters**

Creating the main document.

   and the **Active Window** to use the MERGE document
   Click the **Get Data** button and **Create Data Source**
   Click **OK** to use all the field names present

Creating the data source.

   Type **ADDRESS** as the File name, select to Save in the **3 ½ Floppy (A:)** folder and then **Save**
   Click to **Edit Data Source**
   Type **Mr** (Title) **Peter** (FirstName) **Baxter** (LastName) as the 1st record as shown below, then click **Add New**

MOVING THE CURSOR IN THE DATA FORM

It is necessary to use the TAB key to move from field to field in the data Form.

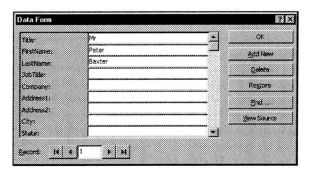

Type **Mr Mukesh Bhatt** as the 2nd record then click **Add New**
Type **Mr Peter Kane** as the 3rd record then click **OK**

Completing the main document.

Completing the merge.

In the MERGE document place the cursor in the empty
TO: box
Click the **Insert Merge Field** button and select **Title**
Press the **Spacebar** once
Click the **Insert Merge Field** button and select **FirstName**
Press the **Spacebar** once
Click the **Insert Merge Field** button and select **LastName**
Select **Tools**, **Mail Merge** and then **Merge** and **Merge** again

6. Use **Save As** to save the merged document with the File name **MERGED**.

7. **Print Preview** and **Print** the 3 individually addressed letters.

8. **Close** the document.

by Paul Summers

THE FURNITURE COMPANY

MEMORANDUM

TO:	<<Title>> <<FirstName>> <<Last Name>>
FROM:	Graham Pearson, District Manager
DATE:	May 25, 1997
RE:	Staff Training

The new computer system will be installed at the beginning of next month and staff training will commence on 10th June, 1997. Mrs Sarah Brown will be taking charge of all staff training from that date.

I have spoken to Mrs Brown and she would like to start the training program with the managers. She will then begin the secretaries training in the second week.

Mrs Brown has had a great deal of experience in these matters and I hope that everyone will co-operate with her wishes. She feels that a three week training period should be sufficient to cover the transition from our manual to the computerised system.

Each of the persons the letter is addressed to will appear in the address box when you merge the letter with the data.

c.c. Mr P Baxter, Mr M Bhatt, Mr P Kane.

EXERCISE 20

OBJECTIVES

♦ Distributing the agenda details of a meeting using Mail Merge.

INSTRUCTIONS

1. **Open** 🖼 the document **AGENDA** created in Exercise 14.

2. Delete the names of the persons the memo is addressed to in the TO: box. At the bottom of the memo press **Enter** several times and then type in **c.c. Ms S O'Connor, Mr T Bendon, Miss R Green, Mr P Bowman.**

3. Use Mail Merge to address the same document to the people identified on the memo. Follow the instructions in the previous exercise.

4. Use **Save As** to save the main letter with the File name **MERGE2**, the data source with the File name **ADDRESS2** and the merged document with the File name **MERGED2**.

5. **Print Preview** 🔍 and **Print** 🖨 the 4 individually addressed letters.

6. **Close** ❎ the document.

THE FURNITURE COMPANY

MEMORANDUM

TO:	<<Title>> <<FirstName>> <<Last Name>>
FROM:	Graham Pearson, District Manager
DATE:	Friday 19th May 1997 at 1500 hrs, Conference Room.
RE:	Weekly status meeting of the Senior Management Committee.

There will be a short meeting of the senior Management Committee this Friday. The Agenda for the meeting is as follows:

1. Minutes of previous meeting.[1]

2. Weekly sales figures.

3. Details of staff training day.[2]

4. Responsibilities on stock taking day.

5. Any other business.

Each of the persons the memo is addressed to will appear in the address box.

c.c. Ms S O'Connor, Mr T Bendon, Miss R Green, Mr P Bowman.

[1] The minutes will be available in the next few days.
[2] Further details will be sent to you before the meeting. Please read.

EXERCISE 21

OBJECTIVES

♦ Creating Mailing Labels using Mail Merge.

INSTRUCTIONS

1. Open a **New** 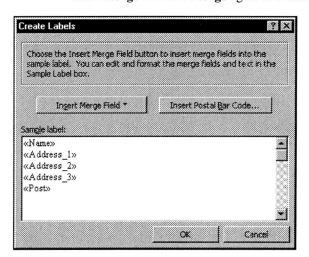 document.

2. Create mailing labels using a customer data file that was imported from Microsoft Access.

   CREATING MAILING LABELS
   Select **Tools** and **Mail Merge**
   Click the **Create** Main document button, select **Mailing Labels** and to use the **Active Window**
   Click **Get Data, Open Data Source**, Look in **3 ½ Floppy (A:)** folder, type **CUSTOMER** as the File name, click to **Open**
   Click to **Set Up Main Document**
   Select the Label products option **Avery A4 and A5 sizes**, the Product number **L7159 - Address**, and then click **OK**
   Click **Insert Merge Field** then **Name**, press **Enter** for a new line
   Click **Insert Merge Field** then **Address_1**, press **Enter**
   Click **Insert Merge Field** then **Address_2**, press **Enter**
   Click **Insert Merge Field** then **Address_3**, press **Enter**
   Click **Insert Merge Field** then **Post**, click **OK** to finish
   Click **Merge** and then **Merge** again to create the mailing labels

3. **Save** 🖫 the mailing labels with the File name **Customer Labels**.

4. **Print Preview** 🔍 and **Print** 🖨 the document.

5. **Close** ✕ the document.

by Paul Summers

ATOMICA
79 WESTBOURNE PARK ROAD
NOTTING HILL
LONDON
W2

BLAKEVILLE CONTRACT
FURNISHERS
8 FINWAY COURT
WHIPPENDALE ROAD
WATFORD

CHISWICK COUNTRY PINE
158 CHISWICK HIGH ROAD
CHISWICK
LONDON
W4

EALING FURNITURE LTD
11 BROADWAY BLDGS
BOSTON ROAD
LONDON
W7

LUXURY (EASIFIT) FURNITURE
LTD
NORTH END ROAD
WEMBLEY
MIDDLESEX
HA9

EXERCISE 22

OBJECTIVES

♦ Creating mailing labels using Mail Merge.

INSTRUCTIONS

1. Open a **New** [ ] document.

2. Create mailing labels using a supplier data file that was imported from Microsoft Access.

   CREATING MAILING LABELS
   Select **Tools** and **Mail Merge**
   Click the **Create** Main document button, select **Mailing Labels** and to use the **Active Window**
   Click **Get Data**, **Open Data Source**, Look in the **3 ½ Floppy (A:)** folder, type **SUPPLIER** as the File name, click to **Open**
   Click to **Set Up Main Document**
   Select the Label products option **Avery A4 and A5 sizes**, the Product number **L7159 - Address**, and then click **OK**
   Click **Insert Merge Field** then **Name**, press **Enter** for a new line
   Click **Insert Merge Field** then **Addr1**, press **Enter**
   Click **Insert Merge Field** then **Addr2**, press **Enter**
   Click **Insert Merge Field** then **Addr3**, press **Enter**
   Click **Insert Merge Field** then **Post_Code**, click **OK** to finish
   Click **Merge** and then **Merge** again to create the mailing labels

3. **Save** [ ] the mailing labels with the File name **Supplier Labels**.

4. **Print Preview** [ ] and **Print** [ ] the document.

5. **Close** [ ] the document.

by Paul Summers

ASCOT FURNISHING FABRICS
LTD
16 FIMER ROAD
FULHAM
LONDON
SW6

BIG TABLE FURNITURE
56 GREAT WESTERN ROAD
HAMMERSMITH
LONDON
W11

COUNTY BEDROOMS
37 QUEENS ROAD
WATFORD
MIDDLESEX

FABRIQUE DU METAL
ORGANISATION
63 EVERITT ROAD
HARLESDEN
LONDON
NW10

HEWGRANGE DESIGN LTD
17 WEST WYCOMBE ROAD
HIGH WYCOMBE

SMITHS FURNITURE LTD
204B WATFORD ROAD
CROXLEY GREEN
WATFORD

EXERCISE 23

OBJECTIVES

♦ Creating mailing labels - the easy way.

♦ Creating a mailing label data table - the hard way.

INSTRUCTIONS

1. Open a **New** ☐ document.

2. Create mailing labels.

> *CREATING MAILING LABELS*
> Select **Tools, Envelopes and Labels**, choose the **Labels** tab and then click **New Document**
> If the gridlines do not appear select **Table** and **Show Gridlines**
> Type the names and addresses shown over the page into each of the cells
> **Save** 🖫 the document with the name **Labels**
> **Print** 🖨 the mailing labels document
> **Close** ⊠ the document

3. Create a mailing label data table.

> *CREATING A DATA TABLE*
> Open a **New** ☐ document
> Select **Tools** and **Mail Merge**
> Click the **Create** Main document button, select **Mailing Labels** and to use the **Active Window**
> Click **Get Data**, **Create Data Source**
> Click **Remove Field Name** *repeatedly* until the Field names in header row list box is empty
> Type **Name** and then click **Add Field Name**
> Type **Address_1** and then click **Add Field Name**
> Type **Address_2** and then click **Add Field Name**
> Type **Address_3** and then click **Add Field Name**
> Type **Post** and then click **Add Field Name**
> Then click **OK**
> Type **NEW CUSTOMERS** as the File name, Save in the **3 ½ Floppy (A:)** folder, then click **Save**
> Click **Edit Data Source**
> Enter the names and addresses shown over the page (use the **Tab** key to move from field to field and **Add New** to save each record)
> Click **OK** to save the addresses entered

Name	Address_1	Address_2	Address_3	Post
ABC GRAPHICS	LOWER REGENT ST	MAYFAIR	LONDON	EC1 2AD
HOMEPRIDE FURNISHERS LTD	101 HIGH ROAD	WILLESDEN	LONDON	NW10
JENNINGS HOUSE FURNISHERS	54 SHENLEY ROAD	BOREHAMWOOD	HERTS	WD6
PHILLIPS & AGNESE FABRICS LTD	ACTON HILL	GUNNERSBURY LANE	LONDON	W3
SHARPS BEDROOM DESIGN	ALPINE HOUSE	HONEYPOT LANE	LONDON	NW9
SINCLAIR LTD	421 EDGWARE ROAD	CRICKLEWOOD	LONDON	NW9
MS C WILSON	27 HIGH ROAD	SOUTHWARK	LONDON	SE2 4CD
ZAMORA	330 PORTOBELLO ROAD	NOTTING HILL	LONDON	W10
ZODIAC FURNITURE LTD	158A BLYTHE ROAD	WESTBOURNE PARK	LONDON	W14

4.   Merge the data table into a mailing label list.

Select **Tools** and **Mail Merge**
Select **Get Data**, **Open Data Source**, type **NEW CUSTOMERS**
as the File name, Look in the **3 ½ Floppy (A:)** folder, click **Open**
Click **Yes** to save the main document
Click to **Set Up Main Document**
Select the Label products option **Avery A4 and A5 sizes**, the
Product number **L7159 - Address**, and then click **OK**
Click **Insert Merge Field** then **Name**, press **Enter** for a new line
Click **Insert Merge Field** then **Address_1**, press **Enter**
Click **Insert Merge Field** then **Address_2**, press **Enter**
Click **Insert Merge Field** then **Address_3**, press **Enter**
Click **Insert Merge Field** then **Post**, click **OK** to finish
Click **Merge** and then **Merge** again to create the mailing labels

5.   **Save** the mailing labels with the File name **New Customer Labels**.

6.   **Print Preview** and **Print** the document.

7.   **Close** each of the documents.

EXERCISE 24

OBJECTIVES

♦ Writing a report on 4 new stock items introduced to last year's catalogue.

♦ Using Tab, Indent, Bullets, Tables and Borders to enhance the report's appearance.

INSTRUCTIONS

1. Open a **New** document.

2. Type in the report as it appears on pages 58 & 59. Sections 3, 4 and 5 below explain certain features.

3. Enhance sections of the text using Tab and Indent for the section of text shown.

   256/1712   Carpenter's Wall Clock
   600/2095   Pine Kitchen Table
   645/1732   Lounge Unit in Black Ash
   645/1749   Lounge Unit in Mahogany

   USING TAB AND INDENT
   Type **256/1712**, press the **Tab** key and then type **Carpenter's Wall Clock** and then **Enter**
   Type **600/2095**, press the **Tab** key and then type the text
   Repeat for the final two stock items
   Highlight the 4 lines of text by **dragging** the pointer across them
   Click the **Increase Indent** button on the toolbar *twice*

4. Enhance sections of the text using Bullets for the section of text shown.

   • Sold very well all through the year.
   • The supplier has always been able to meet supply deadlines.
   • The item was always available in stock.

   USING BULLETS
   Type the 3 lines of text
   Highlight the 3 lines of text by **dragging** the pointer across them
   Click the **Bullets** button on the toolbar

5.   Enhance sections of text using Tables.

CREATING A TABLE
Select **Table**, **Insert Table**, choose the correct number of rows and columns and then click **OK**
Type the required text in the appropriate cells
To make text bold/centred highlight the text in the cell, then click the **Bold** **B** and/or **Center** ☰ button on the toolbar
To shade a cell place the cursor in the cell then select **Format**, **Borders and Shading**, choose the **Shading** tab, change the Patterns Style to **10%**

Name	Addr-1	Addr-2	Post Code
ASCOT FURNISHING FABRICS LTD	16 FIMER ROAD	FULHAM	SW6

6.   **Save** 🖫 the report with the File name **REPORT**.

7.   **Print Preview** 🔍 and **Print** 🖨 the document.

8.   **Close** ✖ the document.

SUMMARY

Four new products were included in last years catalogue. Two, the Carpenter's Wall Clock and the Pine Kitchen Table, performed as expected and will remain as part of our product offer. The Lounge Unit in Black Ash performed poorly and will be replaced with a similar product. The fourth new product, the Lounge Unit in Mahogany, performed below expectations but was recommended to remain as part of the product range but would be purchased from a new supplier.

INTRODUCTION

The Furniture Company added four new products to its catalogue for the sales year commencing October 1996. These were as follows:

256/1712	Carpenter's Wall Clock
600/2095	Pine Kitchen Table
645/1732	Lounge Unit in Black Ash
645/1749	Lounge Unit in Mahogany

All four items were keenly priced against similar products by our major competitors and it was felt that they would all succeed and remain a part of our product range for at least the next 5 years.

REPORT ON NEW STOCK ITEMS

STOCK ITEM - 256/1712

The Carpenter's Wall Clock.

- Sold very well all through the year.
- The supplier has always been able to meet supply deadlines.
- The item was always available in stock.

Stock Code	256/1712
Description	CARPENTER'S WALL CLOCK
Sell Price	£56.99
VAT Rate	1
Last Cost	£47.49
Bought	100
Sold	89

Name	Addr-1	Addr-2	Post Code
ASCOT FURNISHING FABRICS LTD	16 FIMER ROAD	FULHAM	SW6

STOCK ITEM - 600/2095

The Pine Kitchen Table.

- Sold very well all through the year.
- The supplier has always been able to meet supply deadlines.
- The item was always available in stock.

Stock Code	600/2095
Description	PINE KITCHEN TABLE
Sell Price	£125.99
VAT Rate	1
Last Cost	£104.99
Bought	150
Sold	135

Name	Addr-1	Addr-2	Post Code
BIG TABLE FURNITURE	56 GREAT WESTERN ROAD	HAMMERSMITH	W11

STOCK ITEM - 645/1732

The Lounge Unit in Black Ash.

- Sold intermittently through the year.
- The supplier has not always been able to meet supply deadlines.
- The item was not always available in stock.

Stock Code	645/1732
Description	LOUNGE UNIT IN BLACK ASH
Sell Price	£144.99
VAT Rate	1
Last Cost	£120.83
Bought	80
Sold	46

Name	Addr-1	Addr-2	Post Code
COUNTY BEDROOMS	37 QUEENS ROAD	WATFORD	

STOCK ITEM - 645/1749

The Lounge Unit in Mahogany.

- Sold reasonably well all through the year.
- The supplier has nearly always been able to meet supply deadlines.
- The item was generally available in stock.

Stock Code	645/1749
Description	LOUNGE UNIT IN MAHOGANY
Sell Price	£144.99
VAT Rate	1
Last Cost	£120.83
Bought	100
Sold	78

Name	Addr-1	Addr-2	Post Code
HEWGRANGE DESIGN LTD	17 WEST WYCOMBE ROAD	HIGH WYCOMBE	

CONCLUSIONS

The results on the sale of the four new items included in this years product range show that 2 items, 256/1712 and 600/2095, have performed as expected and should be kept in the range for next year. Item 645/1749 has sold reasonably well but has suffered from poor supply. It is recommended that an alternative supplier is used. Item 645/1732 has not sold as anticipated and it is recommended that a replacement product is used.

EXERCISE 25

OBJECTIVES

♦ Enhancing the report's appearance using Styles, Page Numbering and Hard Page Breaks.

INSTRUCTIONS

1. **Open** 📂 the **REPORT** document.

2. Use styles to format all the section headings the same.

    USING STYLES
    Highlight the **SUMMARY** heading at the start of the report
    Change the Font to **Arial**, the Font Size to **14**pt and click the **Bold**
    button on the toolbar | Arial ▼ | 14 ▼ | **B** |
    Click in the Style box to the left of the formatting toolbar type
    SECTIONHEADING | SECTIONHEA ▼ | and then **Enter**
    Highlight the **INTRODUCTION** heading and then select
    SECTIONHEADING in the Style box
    Highlight the **REPORT ON NEW STOCK ITEMS** heading and
    then select **SECTIONHEADING** in the Style box
    Highlight the **CONCLUSIONS** heading and then select
    SECTIONHEADING in the Style box

3. Use styles to format all the stock item headings the same.

    USING STYLES
    Highlight the **STOCK ITEM - 256/1712** heading
    Change the Font to **Arial**, the Font Size to **12**pt and click the **Bold**
    button on the toolbar | Arial ▼ | 12 ▼ | **B** |
    Click in the Style box, type **STOCKHEADING**
    | STOCKHEADI ▼ | and then **Enter**
    Highlight the **STOCK ITEM - 600/2095** heading and then select
    STOCKHEADING in the Style box
    Highlight the **STOCK ITEM - 645/1732** heading and then select
    STOCKHEADING in the Style box
    Highlight the **STOCK ITEM 645/1749** heading and then select
    STOCKHEADING in the Style box

4.   Break the document up into separate pages using the hard page break.

> *USING HARD PAGE BREAK*
> Place the cursor at the *start* of the section heading
> INTRODUCTION and hold the **Ctrl** key and press **Enter**
> Place the cursor at the *start* of the section heading REPORT ON
> NEW STOCK ITEMS and hold the **Ctrl** key and press **Enter**
> Place the cursor at the *start* of the section heading STOCK
> ITEM - 600/2095 and hold the **Ctrl** key and press **Enter**
> Place the cursor at the *start* of the section heading STOCK
> ITEM - 645/1732 and hold the **Ctrl** key and press **Enter**
> Place the cursor at the *start* of the section heading STOCK
> ITEM - 645/1749 and hold the **Ctrl** key and press **Enter**
> Place the cursor at the *start* of the section heading
> CONCLUSIONS and hold the **Ctrl** key and press **Enter**
> N.B. *There should now be 7 pages to the Report.*

5.   Number the pages.

> *USING PAGE NUMBERING*
> Select **Insert**, **Page Numbers** and then **OK**

6.   **Save** ⊞ the report with the File name **REPORT**.

7.   **Print Preview** 🔍 and **Print** 🖨 the document.

8.   **Close** ✖ the document.

EXERCISE 26

OBJECTIVES

♦ Further enhancing the report's appearance by using Headers, Footers and Footnotes.

INSTRUCTIONS

1. **Open** 📂 the **REPORT** document.

2. To read about Headers and Footers click **Help**; **Contents and Index**; **Contents**; *double-click* **Changing the Appearance of Your Page**; *double-click* **Creating and Positioning Headers and Footers**; *double-click* **Headers and footers**. Read the various Word Help topics and then close the Word Help window by clicking the **Close** ❌ Window button.

3. Place a header at the top right of each page of the report.

   USING HEADERS
   Select **View** and **Header and Footer**
   Type **The Furniture Company - Stock Report 1996/97**
   Highlight the text just entered and click the **Bold** 🅱 button and
   the **Align Right** ▤ button on the toolbar
   Click to **Close** the Header window

4. Place a footer at the bottom left of each page of the report.

   USING FOOTERS
   Select **View** and **Header and Footer**
   Click the **Switch Between Header and Footer** 🗗 button
   Type **by Graham Pearson**
   Highlight the text just entered and click the **Bold** 🅱 button and
   the **Italic** 𝐼 button on the toolbar
   Click to **Close** the Footer window

5.   Place footnotes referring to new suppliers.

> *USING FOOTNOTES*
> Move the cursor to page 5 - Stock item 645/1732
> Place the cursor just after the words COUNTY BEDROOMS
> Select **Insert, Footnote**, choose to Insert a **Footnote**, then click **OK**
> Type **BIG TABLE FURNITURE have agreed to supply a replacement item as of October 1997.**
> Move the cursor to page 6 - Stock item 645/1749
> Place the cursor after the words HEWGRANGE DESIGN LTD
> Select **Insert, Footnote**, choose to Insert a **Footnote**, then click **OK**
> Type **BIG TABLE FURNITURE have agreed to supply this item as of October 1997.**

6.   **Save** the report with the File name **REPORT**.

7.   **Print Preview** and **Print** the document.

8.   **Close** the document.

EXERCISE 27

OBJECTIVES

♦ Creating a Contents page for the report.

INSTRUCTIONS

1. **Open** the **REPORT** document.

2. Create a contents page for the report automatically.

TABLE OF CONTENTS
Place the cursor at the END of the document on a NEW PAGE
Select **Insert**, **Index and Tables** and **Table of Contents**
Select **Options**, delete the **1**, **2**, and **3** next to Heading 1, Heading
2, and Heading 3 respectively
Scroll down to the bottom of the Available styles table and
type **1** and **2** next to SECTIONHEADING and
STOCKHEADING respectively, click **OK** and **OK**

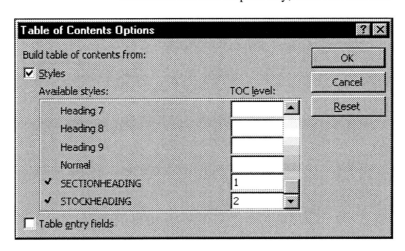

3. Save the contents page as a separate document.

SAVING THE CONTENTS PAGE AS A SEPARATE DOCUMENT
Highlight the Table of Contents generated by **dragging** the pointer
across the text

Click the **Copy**  button on the toolbar

Click the **New** document button on the toolbar

Click the **Paste** button on the toolbar

Select **File**, **Save**, type **CONTENTS** as the File name and
then click **Save**

4.   **Print Preview** [icon] and **Print** [icon] the CONTENTS page.

5.   **Close** [icon] the documents.

EXERCISE 28

OBJECTIVES

♦ Adding a front cover to the report.

♦ Inserting one document after another (merging files).

INSTRUCTIONS

1. **Open** ⬜ the **CONTENTS** document.

2. With the cursor at the start of the page hold down the **Ctrl** key and then press **Enter** to create a new first page.

3. Enter the front cover details of the report on the new first page, see over the page.

4. **Save** ⬜ the changes made to the document.

5. **Print Preview** ⬜ and **Print** ⬜ the document.

6. Merge two files together.

    INSERTING A FILE
    With the **CONTENTS** document open move the cursor to the end of the document
    Select **Insert**, **Break**, **Next page** and **OK**
    Select **Insert**, **File**, type **REPORT** and **OK**
    N.B. *The Report now starts at page 3 but the Contents page list the page numbers starting at page 1.*
    ADJUSTING THE PAGE NUMBERING IN SEC 2
    Place the cursor in **Sec 2** of the document (see bottom left corner of the screen) N.B. *Any page of the main report should be in Section 2 of the document.*
    Select **Insert**, **Page Numbers**, **Format**, Page numbering to **Start at** page 1, then click **OK** and **OK** to save the changes
    N.B. *The page numbering should now be in agreement with the details on the Contents page again.*

7. **Print Preview** ⬜ and **Print** ⬜ the document.

8. Use **Save As** to save the combined document with the File name **COMPLETED REPORT**.

9. **Close** ⬜ the documents.

ADDITIONAL EXERCISE

I.   **Open** 🗁 the document called **LIFEPLAN**.

II.   The document needs to be broken into 13 separate pages. Use **Ctrl Enter** to insert page breaks. The headings for each new page are all in uppercase - INTRODUCTION, JOINING THE PLAN, etc.

III. Use a style of **14pt Arial Bold** for each of the page headings.

IV. Use a style of **12pt Bold** for each of the section headings on each page - on the 1st page these are Eligibility, Joining and Opting-Out & Rejoining.

V.   Create a header with the title **The Furniture Company Life Assurance & Pension Plan**.

VI. Number the pages.

VII. Create a Contents page and a suitable Front Cover of your own design.

This text is Times New Roman, 28pt, Bold and Centred. Note the spacing between each character.

T H E

F U R N I T U R E

C O M P A N Y

The logo is placed in a Text Box which is 10cm by 8cm.

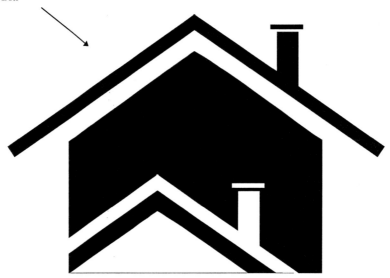

This text is Times New Roman, 18pt, Bold and Centred.

STOCK REPORT 1996/97

by

This text is Times New Roman, 14pt, Bold and Centred.

Graham Pearson

EXERCISE 29

OBJECTIVES

   ♦   Producing a simple Advert.

INSTRUCTIONS

1.   Open a **New** ▢ document.

2.   Type in the text as shown over the page. Use the minus key (---) and the full stop key (...) to create the tear-off form at the bottom of the page.

3.   **Save** ▣ the document with the File name **ADVERT 1**.

4.   **Print Preview** ▣ and **Print** ▣ the document.

5.   **Close** ▣ the document.

THE FURNITURE COMPANY

190/196 The High Street
Willesden
London
NW10 3XD
Tel: 0181 459 0011

November 1996

Dear Customer

Re: 1996 WINTER SALE

We are writing to tell you of this Winter's Sale which starts on the 1st of December.

As one of our best trade customers we know that you will be interested in a special Trade Day Winter Sale which takes place on the 30th of November.

The opening time for Trade customers will be 10.00 am. A buffet lunch will be provided from 12.00 am onwards.

Please complete the tear off slip provided below for your FREE complementary tickets.

Yours sincerely

Mrs P Baxter
Sales Manager

- -

Name..

Address...

....

Post Code...

I would like ..... tickets to the Trade Day Winter Sale.

by Paul Summers

EXERCISE 30

OBJECTIVES

♦ Producing a more complicated advert.

INSTRUCTIONS

1. Open a **New** ⬜ document.

2. Create the heading using a Text Box.

   USING TEXT BOXES
   Select **Insert** and then **Text Box**
   Draw a small box in the *top left corner* of the page by **dragging** the mouse across the page
   FORMATTING A TEXT BOX
   Click on the outline of the box so that the 8 small boxes (handles) appear around the Text Box
   Select **Format** and **Text Box**
   REMOVE THE BORDER LINE AROUND THE TEXT BOX
   Choose the **Colors and Lines** tab, select Line Color **No Line**
   SET THE SIZE OF THE TEXT BOX
   Choose the **Size** tab, set the Height to **2.5 cm**, set the Width to **12.5 cm**
   SET THE POSITION OF THE TEXT BOX
   Choose the **Position** tab
   Set the Horizontal position **0 cm** From the *left* **Margin**
   Set the Vertical position **0 cm** From the *top* **Margin**
   SET THE INTERNAL MARGINS OF THE TEXT BOX
   Choose the **Text Box** tab
   Set the Internal margin Left to **0 cm**
   Set the Internal margin Right to **0 cm**
   Set the Internal margin Top to **0 cm**
   Set the Internal margin Bottom to **0 cm**
   ACCEPTING THE SETTINGS
   Click **OK** to save the changes

PLACING A 3pt BORDER ON THE TOP AND BOTTOM
Select **Format** and then **Borders and Shading**
Change the Width to **3pt** line thickness
Click on the Preview screen to place two lines one at the **Top**
and another at the **Bottom** of the Text Box
Then click **OK**

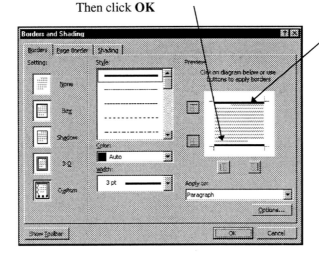

Click inside the box
Type the text "THE FURNITURE COMPANY *Taking care of your needs*" as shown over the page

3. Create a 1.6 cm by 2.5cm Text Box to the right of this one to place the Company logo in. Type the rest of the text as shown with the appropriate formatting. The divider graphic should be on your disc with the File name **DIVIDER**.

4. **Save** the document with the File name **ADVERT 2**.

5. **Print Preview** and **Print** the document.

6. **Close** the document.

Arial, 22pt and Bold

Times, 18pt, Bold & Italic

THE FURNITURE COMPANY

Taking care of your needs

Arial, 36pt, Bold, Centred with character spacing

W I N T E R   S A L E

Times, 12pt

Here at The Furniture Company you will find hundreds of branded products at cut prices in our Winter Sale. We have specially selected products from our catalogue and cut their prices so that you can buy some real bargains. But hurry because at these low prices some bargains may not last too long and the sale must end on the 21st of December.

Don't forget that our new catalogue is available from the 12th of December.

Italic

Discounted items include

Bullets with a 2.5cm Indent & Double line spacing

- A wide range of kitchen equipment

- Bedroom furniture

- A range of home office equipment and furniture

- D-I-Y tools

Picture DIVIDER

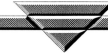

Times, 18pt, Bold & Centred

SALE COMMENCES
9.00am Saturday 1st of December

Times, 18pt, Bold, Centred & Italic

Don't be late!

Times, 12pt, Bold & Centred

**190/196 The High Street, Willesden, London, NW10 3XD.
Tel: 0181 459 0011.**

EXERCISE 31

OBJECTIVES

♦ Producing a simple Flyer.

♦ Using Landscape mode.

♦ Setting Margins, Indenting and using Tables.

INSTRUCTIONS

1. Open a **New** ☐ document.

2. Set up the page for landscape mode.

   USING LANDSCAPE MODE
   Select **File**, **Page Setup**, choose the **Margins** tab, set the Left margin **2.5 cm** and the Right margin **2.5 cm**, choose the **Paper Size** tab, set Orientation to **Landscape**, then click **OK**

3. Use tables to split the page into two.

   INSERTING A TABLE
   Select **Table**, **Insert Table**, set the Number of columns to **2**, set the Number of rows to **1**, then click **OK**
   Select **Format**, **Borders and Shading**, choose the **Borders** tab, change the Setting to **None** and then click **OK**
   Select **Table** and then **Show Gridlines**
   N.B. *The gridlines, unlike the borders, do not print.*
   CREATING A CENTRE MARGIN
   Place the cursor in the left column of the table
   Select **Format**, **Paragraph**, choose the **Indents and Spacing** tab, set the Indentation Right **2.5 cm**, then **OK**
   Place the cursor in the right column of the table
   Select **Format**, **Paragraph**, choose the **Indents and Spacing** tab, set the Indentation Left **2.5 cm**, then **OK**

4. Type in the text as shown over the page.

5. **Save** 🖬 the document with the File name **INVITE 1**.

6. **Print Preview** 🔍 and **Print** 🖨 the document.

7. **Close** ✖ the document.

by Paul Summers

THE

FURNITURE

COMPANY

190/196 The High Street
Willesden
London
NW10 3XD

Tel: 0181 459 0011
Fax: 0181 459 0022

EXERCISE 32

OBJECTIVES

♦ Producing a simple flyer.

♦ Using Landscape mode.

INSTRUCTIONS

1. **Open** the document **INVITE 1**.

2. Delete the text in the two columns of the table.

3. Type in the text as shown over the page.

4. Use **Save As** to save the document with the File name **INVITE 2**.

5. **Print Preview** and **Print** the document.

6. Place the documents INVITE 1 and INVITE 2 back to back and then fold in two to create the invite.

7. **Close** the document.

TRADE DAY

WINTER SALE

1st December 1995
10.00am

Ms Wilson

EXERCISE 33

OBJECTIVES

♦ Producing an advertisement using newspaper style Columns.

♦ Using the Continuous Break command.

INSTRUCTIONS

1. Open a **New** document.

2. Set the page margins to 1cm all around.

   USING PAGE SETUP
   Select **File**, **Page Setup**, choose the **Margins** tab, make the
   Top margin **1 cm**, Bottom margin **1 cm**, Left margin **1 cm**,
   Right margin **1 cm**, and then click **OK**

3. Create the heading in reverse video (i.e. white text).

   REVERSE VIDEO
   Type the text *The* **FURNITURE COMPANY**
   Press the **Enter** key 2 or 3 times
   Highlight the text *The* **FURNITURE COMPANY**, set the Font
   Size to **36pt**, click the **Bold** **B** and **Center** ☰ buttons,
   select **Format**, **Borders and Shading**, choose the **Shading** tab,
   click the Fill color **Black**, and then click **OK**
   N.B. *The text is now black in a black box.*

   With the text still highlighted click the **Font Color**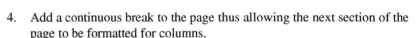

   button and change the text to **White**
   Add the text **New product release** on the next line with **20pt** size

4. Add a continuous break to the page thus allowing the next section of the
   page to be formatted for columns.

   INSERTING A CONTINUOUS BREAK
   Press the down arrow cursor key ↓ to move the cursor out
   of the heading
   Select **Insert**, **Break**, **Continuous** and then **OK**
   N.B. *The document is now in 2 sections. The heading is in
   Sec 1, the rest of the text (to be added) will be in Sec 2 - see
   bottom left corner of the screen.*

by Paul Summers

5. To read about Columns click **Help**; **Contents and Index**; **Contents**; *double-click* **Changing the Appearance of Your Page**; *double-click* **Positioning Text Using Newspaper Columns**; *double-click* **Newspaper columns**. Read the various Word Help topics and then close the Word Help window by clicking the **Close** ☒ Window button.

6. Create a newspaper type column.

    CREATING COLUMNS
    With the cursor in **Sec 2** of the document
    Select **Format, Columns**, Presets **Two** and then **OK**

7. Type in the text as shown over the page. Use Bold, Italic and Tabs where necessary. Click the **Justify** full ▤ button on the toolbar before typing any text to give the text a newspaper type feel. The clock can be inserted by selecting **Insert, File**, highlight **3 ½ Floppy (A:)** folder in the Look in box, type **CLOCK** and click **Open**.

8. **Save** 💾 the document with the File name **NEWS**.

9. **Print Preview** 🔍 and **Print** 🖨 the document.

AMENDMENTS

I. Change the number of columns displayed.

    CHANGING THE NUMBER OF COLUMNS
    Select **Format, Column**, Presets **Three**, and then **OK**

II. Try changing the number of columns back to **Two**, to **Left** and to **Right**. **Print Preview** 🔍 each new option to see how it looks.

III. **Close** ☒ the document.

The FURNITURE COMPANY
New product releases

NEW PRODUCTS

The Furniture Company has added four new products to its catalogue for the year commencing October 1995. These are as follows:

256/1712 Carpenter's Wall Clock
600/2095 Pine Kitchen Table
645/1732 Lounge Unit in Black Ash
645/1749 Lounge Unit in Mahogany

All four items are keenly priced against similar products by our major competitors and we feel that you will find that they will sell well.

STOCK ITEM - 256/1712

The Carpenter's Wall Clock.

The Carpenter's Wall Clock is available in a range of different colours to suite all available tastes and environments.

The internal mechanisms are made to the highest standards with a Quartz crystal that is accurate to one second error every 10 years.

STOCK ITEM - 600/2095

The Pine Kitchen Table.

This solid pine kitchen table is available in both natural and antique finishes. A unique anti-scratch lacquer only available to the Furniture Company protects the surface.

This fine table can also be purchased with a set of matching chairs and would look at home in any dinning room in the land.

STOCK ITEM - 645/1732

The Lounge Unit in Black Ash.

The Lounge Unit has a range of features which include four deep draws and adjustable shelving that can vary from 6" to 20" in height. With its black ash textured finish this unit can be matched with the furnishings in most modern homes.

STOCK ITEM - 645/1749

The Lounge Unit in Mahogany.

This unit is the same as item 645/1732 as detailed above except that the finish is mahogany veneer. This unit has the same adjustable shelf features as the Lounge Unit in Black Ash.

FURTHER DETAILS

For further details of the above items please contact our Sales Manager Mr P Kane at:

The Furniture Company, 190/196 The High Street, Willesden, London, NW10 3XD. Tel: 0181 459 0011.

Name_____

Address_____

by Paul Summers

EXERCISE 34

OBJECTIVES

♦ Producing a blank Order Form.

INSTRUCTIONS

1. Open a **New** ⬜ document.

2. Set the left and right margins to **1 cm**.

3. Type in the text as shown over the page.

   THE ORDER GRID
   Select **Table**, **Insert Table**, include **5** Columns and **7** Rows,
   then click **OK**

   Use the double line double arrow ◀▐▶ pointer to change
   the width of the columns
   Use the **Format, Borders and Shading**, and the **Borders** tab
   to remove some of the border lines
   Use the **Format, Borders and Shading**, and the **Shading** tab
   to add the shading
   For the entry **Orders in excess of £75 ......** highlight two adjacent
   cells and select **Table** and **Merge Cells**

   THE SPECIAL OFFER
   Add **Borders** with a **3pt** line top & bottom, and set the Patterns
   Style to **10%** shading

   DELIVERY & RETURN ADDRESS
   Select **Table, Insert Table**, include **2** Columns and **1** Row,
   then click **OK**
   Select **Format, Paragraph**, **3 cm** Indentation Left and **OK**
   for *both* columns
   Use the **underscore** key (Shift Minus) to draw the horizontal lines

4. **Save** 💾 the document with the File name **ORDER**.

5. **Print Preview** 🔍 and **Print** 🖨 the document.

6. **Close** ✖ the document.

ORDER FORM

Please despatch the following items ASAP:

ITEM	STOCK CODE	Qty	PRICE	TOTAL
Orders in excess of £75.00 - *For orders in excess of £75 postage and packaging is FREE.*			**Plus p&p per order**	£3.00
			Total order value	

SPECIAL OFFER

Purchase items in value in excess of £200 and receive a £30 voucher to spend on the item(s) of your choice.

DELIVERY ADDRESS:

Mr/Mrs/Miss/Ms_____

Address_____

_____

_____

Postcode_____

Signature_____Date_____

RETURN ORDER TO:

I enclose a cheque/postal order for £_____ made payable to **The Furniture Company** @

190/196 The High Street
Willesden
London
NW10 3XD

by Paul Summers

EXERCISE 35

OBJECTIVES

♦   Producing a blank Invoice.

INSTRUCTIONS

1.   Open a **New** ☐ document.

2.   Type in the text as shown over the page. Use tables for the various sections of the page:

Your Order No:/Invoice No: (**3** rows by **4** columns),
To: and From: (**2** rows by **4** columns),
and the Order Details section (**9** rows by **5** columns).

3.   **Save** 🖫 the document with the File name **INVOICE**.

4.   **Print Preview** 🔍 and **Print** 🖨 the document.

5.   **Close** ✖ the document.

INVOICE

Your Order No:		**Invoice No:**		
Date:		**Date:**		
Ref:		**Ref:**		

To:

From:
The Furniture Company
190/196 The High Street
Willesden
London
NW10 3XD

ORDER DETAILS:

ITEM	STOCK CODE	Qty	PRICE	TOTAL

Make cheques payable to - *The Furniture Company plc.*	**Plus p&p per order**	£3.00
	Total order value	

EXERCISE 36

OBJECTIVES

♦ Producing a blank Delivery Note.

INSTRUCTIONS

1. **Open** 📂 the document **INVOICE**.

2. Modify the text as shown over the page. For the Order Details table it will be necessary to delete 2 columns.

   DELETING COLUMNS IN TABLES
   Place the cursor in any one of the columns
   Select **Table** and **Select Column**
   Select **Table**, **Delete Column**
   Repeat the above for one more column
   Change the column headings as shown

3. Use **Save As** to save the document with the File name **DELIVERY**.

4. **Print Preview** 🔍 and **Print** 🖨 the document.

5. **Close** ❎ the document.

DELIVERY NOTE

Your order No: Invoice No:

Date: Date:

Ref: Ref:

To: From:

                                        The Furniture Company
                                        190/196 The High Street
                                        Willesden
                                        London
                                        NW10 3XD

ORDER DETAILS:

ITEM	Qty	RECEIVED (Y/N)

Please sign below to confirm the order has been received and pass on to your Accounts Department so that they can make the necessary payment.

Signature:

Date:

by Paul Summers

EXERCISE 37

OBJECTIVES

♦   Producing a blank Remittance Advice form.

INSTRUCTIONS

1.   **Open** ⬜ either the INVOICE or DELIVERY document.

2.   Create the document as shown over the page by modifying the existing one.

3.   Use **Save As** to save the document with the File name **REMIT**.

4.   **Print Preview** ⬜ and **Print** ⬜ the document.

5.   **Close** ⬜ the document.

REMITTANCE ADVICE

To:

From:

The Furniture Company
190/196 The High Street
Willesden
London
NW10 3XD

Transaction type	Your reference	Date	Amount (£)
Total Remittance			

ADDITIONAL EXERCISES

ADDITIONAL EXERCISE 1

THE FURNITURE COMPANY

190/196 The High Street
Willesden
London
NW10 3XD
Tel: 0181 459 0011

17 August 1997
Our Ref: PK/AHC

Big Table Furniture Co.

Dear Mr Johnson,

YOUR ORDER NUMBER No 2354

Thank you for your letter of the 10th August 1997 concerning your Order No. 2354. Our records show that the order was despatched on the 4th August and as such I would ask that you check your records once again.

Please phone and ask for me personally if the goods have still not arrived and I will arrange for an immediate replacement to be despatched.

Yours sincerely,

Pater Kane
Sales Manager

ADDITIONAL EXERCISE 2

THE FURNITURE COMPANY

190/196 The High Street
Willesden
London
NW10 3XD

12 July 1997
Our Ref: KW/AB

Dear Sally,

JOB ENQUIRY

Than you for your recent letter with regards to vacancies at The Furniture Company.

I would be grateful if you could send me more comprehensive details of the type of work that you have undertaken in the past to complement your CV.

As you are no doubt aware we are a large company selling a diverse range of products and we are currently looking for new staff.

During the next two weeks we will be contacting all candidates for an interview and I look forward to meeting you then.

Should you require further information please don't hesitate to contact my secretary on the number shown below.

Yours sincerely,

Mrs K Williams
Personnel

**The Furniture Company, 190/196 The High Street, Willesden, London, NW10 3XD.
Tel: 0181 459 0011.**

by Paul Summers

ADDITIONAL EXERCISE 3

The Furniture Company

SPRING CLEAROUT SALE

12th April 1997

09.00 - 18.00hrs

**The Furniture Company, 190/196 The High Street, Willesden, London, NW10 3XD.
Tel: 0181 459 0011.**

ADDITIONAL EXERCISE 4

THE FURNITURE COMPANY

AGENDA

A meeting of all Senior Sales Staff will be held on Friday 26th June 1997 at 1500 hrs in the Conference Room.

Matters to be discussed:

1. Apologies for absence.

2. Minutes of last meeting.

3. Results of the "Spring Clearout Sale".

4. Summer sales strategies.

5. A.O.B.

6. Next meeting.

Mr P Kane

ADDITIONAL EXERCISE 5

M E M O R A N D U M

TO:	ALL STAFF
FROM:	Peter Kane
DATE:	Monday 29th June 1997
RE:	SUMMER SALE

As you are all aware next week marks the start of our Summer Sale. Can I please remind all of you that staff training will be undertaken this Friday, the 3rd of July, and that it is imperative that ALL staff attend promptly at 8.30am.

ADDITIONAL EXERCISE 6

The Furniture Company

Issue 12

SUMMER EXCURSION

This year's summer excursion will be to Brighton on the 25th of July.

As usual all employees and their families are invited. The price per person is a very reasonable £10. This includes a meal in the evening on the journey home - fish and chips!

BOOK NOW TO AVOID DISAPPOINTMENT

To book your place(s) phone Tony before 5.0pm Thursday 12th of July.

ART DECO

The latest addition to our product range includes a number of household items in the Art Deco style. These include:

- **Table lighting.**
- **Mirrors.**
- **Coffee tables.**

These items are only available at The Furniture Company having been commissioned from an internationally renowned designer.

The usual staff discounts apply.

GOOD NEWS

Mary in personnel gave birth to a 7lb 4oz baby girl last Wednesday at St Mary's Hospital in Paddington.

Mother and baby are both doing well. Those wishing to sign the congratulations card you will find it in Personnel.

To place any report in the Newsletter please contact:
Tony James, 190/196 The High Street, Willesden, London, NW10 3XD.
Tel: 0181 459 0011. Fax: 0181 459 0022.

by Paul Summers

TOOLBARS - Standard/Formatting

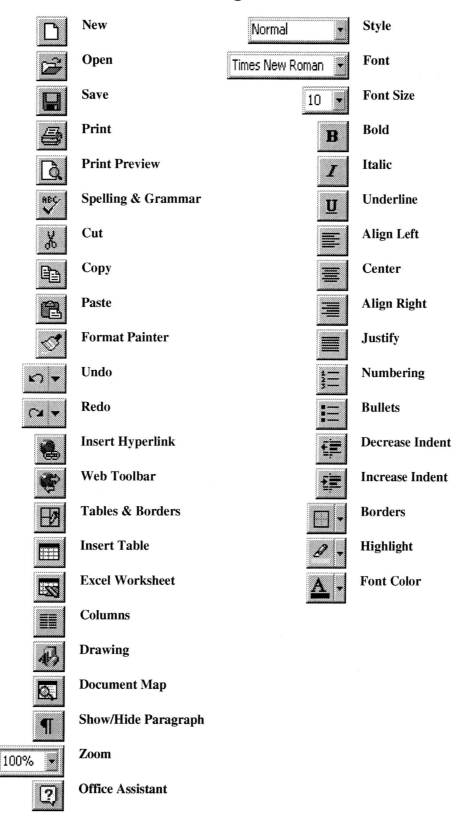

New	Style (Normal)
Open	Font (Times New Roman)
Save	Font Size (10)
Print	Bold
Print Preview	Italic
Spelling & Grammar	Underline
Cut	Align Left
Copy	Center
Paste	Align Right
Format Painter	Justify
Undo	Numbering
Redo	Bullets
Insert Hyperlink	Decrease Indent
Web Toolbar	Increase Indent
Tables & Borders	Borders
Insert Table	Highlight
Excel Worksheet	Font Color
Columns	
Drawing	
Document Map	
Show/Hide Paragraph	
Zoom (100%)	
Office Assistant	

TOOLBARS - Tables & Borders/Drawing

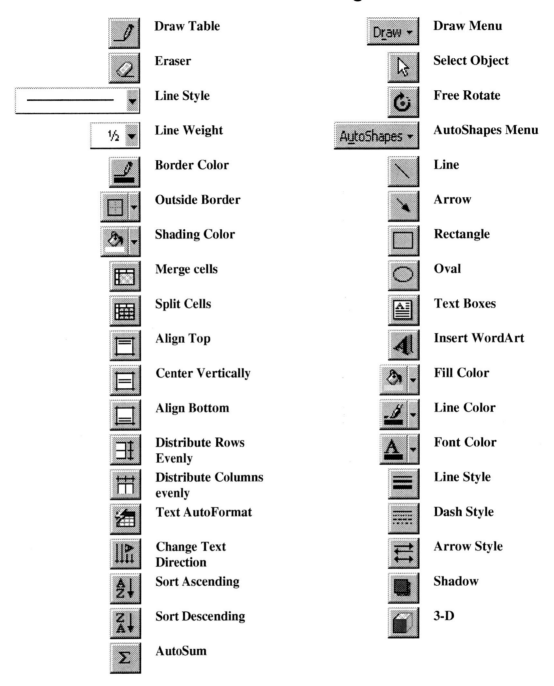

Draw Table	Draw Menu
Eraser	Select Object
Line Style	Free Rotate
Line Weight	AutoShapes Menu
Border Color	Line
Outside Border	Arrow
Shading Color	Rectangle
Merge cells	Oval
Split Cells	Text Boxes
Align Top	Insert WordArt
Center Vertically	Fill Color
Align Bottom	Line Color
Distribute Rows Evenly	Font Color
Distribute Columns evenly	Line Style
Text AutoFormat	Dash Style
Change Text Direction	Arrow Style
Sort Ascending	Shadow
Sort Descending	3-D
AutoSum	

PROOF CORRECTION SYMBOLS

This appendix contains the basic proof correction symbols commonly used to correct and alter printed text.

Instruction	Mark	Example
Insert text at the point indicated	$\wedge$	This $\wedge$ an example. $\wedge$ *is*
Delete the text indicated	δ followed by $/$ or a line through the words	δ This i$\not{s}$ is an example. δ This ~~is~~ is an example.
Do NOT delete the text	dashed underline	Do ~~NOT~~ delete the text.
Change the letter underlined to a capital	$\equiv$	Dr peter Johnson $\equiv$
Change the letter underlined to a lower case	$\not{/}$	DR Peter Johnson $\not{/}$
Connect two paragraphs together		.... to the end. ⌐ Tomorrow is the start of .....
Change words around.		This the is last ...
Start a new paragraph from this point on		... end of the day. You will then
Indent a paragraph by the amount indicated	*0.5"*	*0.5"* The reasons for this are: a) The weather. b) The humidity.
Removing the indent from a paragraph by the amount indicated	*0.5"*	*0.5"* The reasons for this are: a) The weather. b) The humidity.

ORDER FORM

Software Training Workbooks

Name	
Address	
Post Code	
Occupation	Student / Teacher / Other

Workbooks – Single Copies	Price	Qty	Total
Word 97 for Windows Workbook Beginners	£9.95		
Excel 97 for Windows Workbook Beginners	£9.95		
Access 97 for Windows Workbook Beginners	£9.95		
PowerPoint 97 for Windows Workbook Beginners	£9.95		
Publisher 98 for Windows Workbook Beginners	£9.95		
Visual Basic 5.0 for Windows Workbook Beginners	£12.95		
FrontPage 98 for Windows Workbook Beginners	£9.95		
Word 97 for Windows Workbook Advanced	£9.95		
Excel 97 for Windows Workbook Advanced	£9.95		
Access 97 for Windows Workbook Advanced	£9.95		
Publisher 98 for Windows Workbook Advanced	£9.95		
Visual Basic 5.0 for Windows Workbook Advanced	£12.95		
		SUB TOTAL	
		p&p	
		TOTAL	£

This offer is ONLY valid for customers in the UK.

Please add postage & packaging @ £0.50 per book, up to a maximum of £3.50
(i.e. £1.50 for 3 books; £3.50 for 7 books; and £3.50 for 15 books)

Please make all cheques payable to Software Training Workbooks.
Postage charged @£3.50 where Invoicing is requested – business users only.

STW, 16 Nursery Road, Pinner, Middlesex, HA5 2AP.

ORDER FORM

Software Training Workbooks

Name	
Address	
Post Code	
Occupation	Student / Teacher / Other

Workbooks - Single Copies	Price	Qty	Total
Word 2000 for Windows Workbook Beginners	£9.95		
Excel 2000 for Windows Workbook Beginners	£9.95		
Access 2000 for Windows Workbook Beginners	£9.95		
PowerPoint 2000 for Windows Workbook Beginners	£9.95		
Publisher 2000 for Windows Workbook Beginners	£9.95		
Visual Basic 6.0 for Windows Workbook Beginners	£12.95		
FrontPage 2000 for Windows Workbook Beginners	£9.95		
Word 2000 for Windows Workbook Advanced	£9.95		
Excel 2000 for Windows Workbook Advanced	£9.95		
Access 2000 for Windows Workbook Advanced	£9.95		
Publisher 2000 for Windows Workbook Advanced	£9.95		
Visual Basic 6.0 for Windows Workbook Advanced	£12.95		
		SUB TOTAL	
		p&p	
		TOTAL	£

This offer is ONLY valid for customers in the UK.

Please add postage & packaging @ £0.50 per book, up to a maximum of £3.50
(i.e. £1.50 for 3 books; £3.50 for 7 books; and £3.50 for 15 books)

Please make all cheques payable to Software Training Workbooks.
Postage charged @£3.50 where Invoicing is requested - business users only.

STW, 16 Nursery Road, Pinner, Middlesex, HA5 2AP.